# PARTICLE
# PHYSICS
## THE
## HIGH-ENERGY
## FRONTIER

# PARTICLE PHYSICS

## THE HIGH-ENERGY FRONTIER

**M. Stanley Livingston**

*Professor of Physics,*
*Massachusetts Institute of Technology*
*Associate Director, National Accelerator Laboratory*
*Weston, Illinois*

**McGraw-Hill Book Company**
*New York    St. Louis    San Francisco    Toronto    London    Sydney*

# PARTICLE PHYSICS
THE
HIGH-ENERGY
FRONTIER

# PREFACE

This book is an introductory survey of the field of particle physics, intended for students and others who have a general interest in the subject. It was developed from notes for a series of Freshman Research Seminars offered to small groups of first-year students at Harvard University and the Massachusetts Institute of Technology when the author was Director of the Cambridge Electron Accelerator. The subject matter proved to be of considerable interest to these students, many of whom plan to specialize in other fields. Most of the freshmen were well prepared in basic physics and mathematics. They were able to accept and discuss the bases of modern atomic structure and displayed considerable enthusiasm in discussions of the new concepts of particle physics, such as strangeness and antimatter. However, they had not yet attained sufficient facility in mathematics to appreciate advanced theoretical treatments of the field.

The introductory chapters have been expanded beyond the coverage necessary for an advanced physics student to provide an adequate background of those concepts and physical laws developed in classical and atomic physics on which the structure of particle physics is built. These chapters can be passed over quickly by the reader who has mastered these fields. For less-advanced students and for readers from other professional fields, the classical analogies and the early work in these more mature fields will provide a better basis for appreciating the significance of the new concepts required in particle physics.

This survey deals primarily with concepts and with the experimental observations which have led to and which justify these concepts. No attempt is made to present theoretical derivations or methodology, although they have had a major influence on our growing understanding of the field. Wherever possible, however, concepts and conclusions coming from success-ful theoretical advances are described. The author accepts responsibility for any shortcomings or oversimplifications in these descriptions. It is also necessary to introduce some of the new technical terms—the jargon of the field—which are essential if the reader wishes to go more deeply into the field.

This book is not intended as a textbook for advanced students in particle physics; they will find their own sources in the research literature. Detailed references to source material are deliberately omitted. Rather, it is a limited survey of the pertinent facts, terminology, and concepts in this new field of basic research. It may be of value to beginning students and to teachers in other fields of science who want to know "what's going on" in this field. It should be helpful to accelerator physicists and engineers who build the tools and devices needed for high-energy research. For others, it may give some feeling for the mounting excitement among scientists in the field, who sense a significant breakthrough in our understanding of the particles of nature in the not-too-distant future.

M. Stanley Livingston

# CONTENTS

Preface                                                    v

1    Frontiers of Science                                  1
2    The Nuclear Atom                                      9

        The Electron                                       10
        Natural Radioactivity                              15
        Positive Rays and the Proton                       17
        Nuclear Disintegration by $\alpha$ Particles       22
        The Neutron                                        23
        Strong Nuclear Force                               26

3    Quanta and Waves in Atoms                             29

        Atomic Spectra                                     30
        The Bohr Atom                                      32
        Light: Waves or Particles?                         40

Relativistic Concepts 43
Concepts of Wave Mechanics 47
Statistics of Particles 58

**4   Other Elementary Particles** 61

The Positron 62
Neutrinos 65
Mesons 69
Muons 74
Strange Particles 77
Antiparticles 82
Classifications 84

**5   Conservation Laws** 89

Conservation of Energy 90
Conservation of Linear Momentum 94
Conservation of Angular Momentum 100
Angular Momentum of Particles 103
Conservation of Charge 110
Conservation of Particle Number 112

**6   Masses of the Observable Particles** 117

Electrons 118
Protons 120
Neutrons 121
Muons 122
Pions 123
Kaons 126
Hyperons 127

**7   Parity: The Mirror World** 129

Parity 132
Conservation of Parity 135
Breakdown of Parity Conservation 138
Spin Correlations in Weak Interactions 142

**8   Charge Independence and Isotopic Spin** 147

Charge Independence 148
Isotopic Spin 149

Third Component of Isotopic Spin 151
Conservation of Isotopic Spin 152
Nonconservation of Isotopic Spin 154

**9    Strangeness** 157

Associated Production 159
Conservation of Strangeness 160
Properties of Kaons 163
Hypercharge 166

**10   Resonances** 169

Experimental Methods 170
Lifetimes and Widths 177
Baryon Resonances 179
Meson Resonances 181

**11   Exercises in Conservation** 183

Summary of Conservation Laws 185
Strong Interactions 186
Electromagnetic Interactions 192
Weak Interactions 195

**12   Basic Symmetries of Nature** 199

Symmetry of Space 201
Symmetry of Time 204
Symmetry of Spin Permutation 207
Symmetry of Charge Permutation 208
TCP Invariance 210
SU(3) and SU(6) Symmetries 212
Tentative Conclusions 216

**References for Further Reading** 221

**Index** 225

*chapter 1*

# FRONTIERS
# OF SCIENCE

THERE IS IN MANKIND a driving urge to explore the unknown. In past ages much of this exploration was geographical—the search for new continents and new seas. In our generation the most challenging frontiers lie in the search for new knowledge about nature and about man, and the most dramatic progress has been made on the frontiers of science. This quest for knowledge through science has been gathering momentum for centuries, but the pace has increased enormously in the past few decades. New knowledge gained through research has stimulated new industries which have greatly expanded our standard of living. It is no coincidence that this burst of activity in science has been accompanied by a technological revolution which has created a flood of new products and new capabilities. These new capabilities, in turn, provide the scientific laboratories with opportunities for further advances and faster progress.

Within our own lifetimes the whole expanding frontier of science and the related technologies has taken fire. We seem to have passed a critical threshold, and our scientific-technological society seems to have reached the status of a self-sustaining chain reaction. Research is supported by massive government subsidies, not only in national laboratories but also in universities and industrial laboratories. The processes of research, innovation, development, and production feed upon and stimulate one another. The time interval between conception of a new idea and the development of a useful product has been telescoped.

Basic research has been swept up on the tide of this technological revolution. The research fields which have received the largest support are those with the most impressive applications. The present broad program of research in biology and medicine is justified by the dramatic successes in medical applications, such as the use of the new wonder drugs in the control of disease. The rapid application of transistors to electronic devices and the growth of automation in industry have brought large support for basic research in solid-state physics and in electronics, especially in industrial laboratories. The continuing and expanding support for research in nuclear physics is clearly associated with the success of atomic weapons with their tremendous implications for defense and for nuclear power. The space race started by the first Russian Sputnik not only has spurred on the development of satellites and missile guidance systems, but also has stimulated research in astrophysics and enlarged our scientific education programs.

Other fields of basic research that do not have such obvious immediate applications to practical needs have also prospered. The search for new knowledge about nature and the properties of matter has paid such striking dividends in the past that investments in basic research are recognized as essential for future progress, not only by university scholars but also by government officials. Many scientists hold an almost mystical conviction that most scientific advances will ultimately contribute useful products to the benefit of society. But, on a broader level, many of these basic research fields offer challenges which transcend the motivation of usefulness and have their meanings in the capacity for understanding by the human mind. To many research scientists, the intellectual challenge is sufficient motivation and new knowledge is a justification in itself.

Particle physics is one frontier of basic research which excites a tremendous intellectual interest. The purpose of scientists in this field is to determine the physical laws which govern the formation of the basic constituents of matter—the protons, neutrons, and electrons of which this world is made. Particle physics is the study of the origin and properties of the nuclear force which binds protons and neutrons together to form the nuclei of atoms. It is the study of the properties of the individual particles, a search for internal structure (if it exists), a study of the many ways in which energy can condense in the form of mass.

A satisfactory theory of the nuclear force would explain why nature allows only a few of the many known kinds of particles to be stable and why they have their discrete values of mass. The challenge of truly understanding this fundamental law of nature, and how this law governs our material universe, is one of the greatest incentives to the human mind in all history.

This research field has evolved from nuclear physics as the energies available from particle accelerators have grown larger and larger. But it deals with problems of a more fundamental character. Particle physics goes as far beyond nuclear physics as nuclear physics has gone beyond atomic physics. Atomic physics deals with the electronic structure of atoms and with the electromagnetic or "chemical" forces which bind atoms into molecules. These electromagnetic forces vary inversely with the square of the distance between the positively charged nuclei and the negatively charged electrons. The familiar visualization of the atom is a miniature solar system with the nucleus at the center and a cloud of electrons circulating around it in planetary-like orbits. If the atomic diameter were 1 mile, the nucleus would be about the size of a pea, yet it contains 99.5 percent of the mass. The forces binding atoms into molecules come from the sharing of electrons in the outer orbits, and their binding energies are low. The burning of coal releases only about 0.5 electron volts (eV) of energy per atom.

The nuclear force which binds protons and neutrons so tightly is a completely different type of force. It is very strong at the spacings of nucleons within the nucleus and yet is negligible at distances of a few nuclear radii. Nuclear binding energies are very large. The average energy required to separate a single proton or neutron from a nucleus is about 8 million electron volts (MeV), 10 million times greater than the energy to remove an outer electron from an atom. However, nuclei can be disintegrated when sufficiently high-energy particles are used as projectiles, such as those produced by particle accelerators in the energy range from 1 to 20 MeV. Nuclear physicists have learned how to disintegrate essentially all of the stable nuclei, forming new kinds of nuclei with different numbers of protons and neutrons. Many of these new nuclei are unstable and decay radioactively. A great deal has been learned about the structure of nuclei, their interactions, binding energies, and excitation states. We know many of the consequences of the nuclear force, but we do not know its origin.

Atoms come in all sizes, ranging from hydrogen (1 proton in the nucleus) to uranium (92 protons and 146 neutrons). Medium-weight nuclei are the most tightly bound and the most stable. Heavy nuclei like radium, thorium, and uranium are unstable and decay radioactively with the emission of $\alpha$, $\beta$, and $\gamma$ rays; the quantities we observe in nature are the residues of much larger amounts present when the earth was formed.

A few special heavy nuclei such as $U^{235}$ and $Pu^{239}$ are unstable in a different way: when a slow neutron is absorbed they fission into two medium-weight nuclei with the release of tremendous energy as well as several extra neutrons. The energy released from each fission process in an atomic bomb or in a chain-reacting pile is over 200 MeV, or about 1 MeV per particle in the nucleus.

Another special type of interaction is the fusion of light-weight nuclei such as $H^2$, $H^3$, and $Li^6$ into the more stable $He^4$ nuclei plus extra neutrons, with the release of several million electron volts per particle. This interaction is the source of the energy released in thermonuclear reactions and the hydrogen bomb. Intensive study is now being undertaken to discover methods for controlling the production of power through the fusion of such light elements; the production and control of very-high-temperature plasmas is the most promising development at the present time.

In all of these processes the released energy comes from the excess mass which is transformed into energy; the product particles have less mass than the primary particles. We can compute the energy release through the Einstein equivalence relation $E = mc^2$. This mass energy was stored in the heavy nuclei and in the very light nuclei in the form of excess mass at the time our galaxy was formed several billion years ago. We have learned how to trigger this energy release in chain reactions such as fission and fusion; we have learned how to "burn" the excess mass. But we have not learned why nature behaves in this way. Relatively, we know little more about the origin of this stored energy than our prehistoric ancestors knew about the chemical laws governing the emission of heat when they burned fuels such as wood or coal.

Particle physics deals with the structure and properties of the nucleons themselves. It is a new field of science built on and growing out of nuclear physics. The tools are multi-billion-volt accelerators. At the present time there is no known limit, other than cost, to the energies which can be attained with still larger accelerators. Research scientists in the field are clamoring for accelerators of higher and higher energies, and the cost estimates for these gigantic machines are startling to budget planners. Experiments at these energies also require large and costly equipment, such as liquid-hydrogen bubble chambers, massive magnets for momentum analysis, heavy shielding, and fast computers for data analysis. The scale of the equipment is hundreds of times greater than for experiments in nuclear physics. Budgets for research in this new field are enormous compared with the accepted budgets of a few decades ago for basic research. The high-energy frontier has become the financial-support frontier. Paradoxically, the study of the smallest particles in nature requires the largest and most costly instruments. The closest parallel is the field of astrophysics—the frontier of the infinitely large—which also requires massive and costly instruments, such as radio telescopes and manned satellites for space exploration.

The smaller the particles we investigate, and the deeper we probe into these particles, the higher are the energies required. A basic concept of the quantum mechanics, which has been our most successful approach to a theory of matter up to the present, is that very high energies are associated with very small dimensions.   When a beam of high-energy particles is used as a probe for studying other particles, the detail which can be resolved is determined by the associated wavelength of the particles, as it is for optical instruments using visible light.   The de Broglie wavelength of a moving particle varies inversely with particle momentum.   So the higher the energy, the shorter is the wavelength and the sharper is the probe.   Particle physics requires the use of very high energies and very sharp probes.   The high-energy frontier is also the frontier of the infinitesimally small.

No practical applications of particle physics can yet be visualized or predicted with any certainty.   In this respect, science fiction writers are still far ahead of research scientists. But no responsible scientist would attempt to justify support for research in this field with prediction of an "anti-matter engine," or a super "meson bomb," or a "hyper-drive" for spaceships.   There are, of course, many significant and valuable by-products coming from the demand for new technological products and devices.   The scientific requirements for specialty instruments and equipment with new capabilities present a challenge to industry to improve its products.   Large contracts go to commercial engineering firms to develop the massive and costly devices needed for research in this field.   But this type of spin-off of new technology is inherent in many fields and is not unique to particle physics.

Justification for support of this new research field must be found in the value to our society of this new knowledge about nature.   It is *basic* research, and the only product we can expect within our generation is this new knowledge.   However, in the opinion of many qualified observers, we are at the threshold of a significant upward step in human understanding, a quantum jump in our knowledge about nature of a magnitude equivalent to those represented by the theory of relativity or the development of quantum mechanics. Ultimately, the impact will be felt on a very broad intellectual and cultural level. The frontier of high energy and the infinitesimally small is a challenge to the mind of man. If we can reach and cross this frontier, our generation will have furnished a significant milestone in human history.

*chapter 2*

# THE
# NUCLEAR
# ATOM

OUR EXPERIENCE IN THE MACROSCOPIC WORLD, and the early history of science, have predisposed scientists to search for basic simplicities in nature, such as a set of elementary particles of which all composite systems are formed. The concept of atomicity is appealing to the human mind. It was taught by the Greek philosophers in the fourth and fifth centuries B.C. Democritus phrased the atomic hypothesis this way: "The universe consists of empty space and an (almost) infinite number of indivisible and invisible particles which differ from each other in form, position and arrangement." This faith in the underlying simplicity and atomicity of nature has provided the motivation for many scientific advances. The development of the atomic theory, from the early concepts of Dalton and Mendeleev to the modern formulations of the quantum electrodynamics, has justified this faith that nature displays order and structure. In this development, the identification of the elementary components of atoms was an essential first step.

## THE ELECTRON

Faraday's experiments on the electrolysis of aqueous solutions of chemical compounds suggested that electricity is atomic in nature. He found that the amount of electricity needed to deposit 1 equiv wt (1 mole) of a chemical substance was the same for all univalent substances; this quantity of charge is known as the faraday, F. The results implied that an elementary unit of electric charge was associated with each *ion* in solution. Stoney in 1874 suggested the name *electron* for this unit and calculated its magnitude $e$ from the rough value available at that time of Avogadro's number ($N_0$ = the number of molecules per mole), by the relation $F = N_0 e$.

The phenomena of electrical discharge in rarefied gases also provided evidence for the atomicity of electric charge. When a gas is enclosed in a glass tube with two electrodes to which an electric potential is applied, the gas becomes luminous and the spectrum of wavelengths emitted is characteristic of the gas. At low gas pressures ($10^{-4}$ mm Hg), the illumination fades away and a fluorescent glow appears on the glass wall opposite the cathode. When these *cathode rays* are collimated by slits and their properties studied, they are found to carry negative electric charge, to produce ionization in the gas, and to be deflected by transverse electrostatic and magnetic fields. The most reasonable interpretation is that the cathode rays consist of negatively charged particles.

The photoelectric effect discovered by Hertz in 1887 added more evidence. Hertz found, quite accidentally, that the light emitted from one spark would trigger a spark between another nearby pair of electrodes across which a suitable potential was applied, and he concluded that the effect was due to ultraviolet light falling on the electrodes of the second gap. Further work by others showed that light releases negative electric charge from an illuminated metal plate, which can produce a continuous current in a closed circuit with a battery. Again it seemed probable that electrified particles were being emitted.

Still another bit of evidence came from Zeeman's observations in 1896 that spectral lines are split into components when the source emitting the spectrum is placed in a strong magnetic field. Following a suggestion by Lorentz, he found that these components are polarized along different axes. Although the classical theory used by Lorentz to interpret the effect is no longer considered valid, it did include the concept of electrically charged particles moving in circular orbits in the magnetic field.

Final confirmation of the view that cathode rays consist of negatively charged particles came with J. J. Thomson's experiments on the properties of these rays in 1897. In these experiments a well-collimated beam of cathode rays was arranged to traverse a region of crossed electrostatic and magnetic fields, such that the transverse forces on the moving particles due to these fields were opposed and the net deflection was zero. The electric force is given by $eE$, and the magnetic force by $Hev$, where $v$ is particle velocity.  If these forces are equal, we have

$$eE = Hev \qquad \text{or} \qquad v = \frac{E}{H} \tag{2.1}$$

So the magnitudes of the fields provide a measure of the velocity.

Then, if the magnetic field is removed, the deflection of the beam due to the electric field can be used to calculate the charge-to-mass ratio $e/m$ of the particles.   The transverse deflection which is produced by the electric field is due to an acceleration $Ee/m$ acting during a time $l/v$, where $l$ is the length of the region of deflecting field, or

$$s = \frac{1}{2}\frac{Ee}{m}\left(\frac{l}{v}\right)^2 \tag{2.2}$$

The angular deflection, which is the measured quantity, is also given by

$$\tan\theta = \frac{s}{\frac{1}{2}l} \tag{2.3}$$

These relations can be solved for the ratio $e/m$

$$\frac{e}{m} = \frac{v^2}{El}\tan\theta = \frac{E\tan\theta}{H^2 l} \tag{2.4}$$

The value of $e/m$ found by Thomson was $5.1 \times 10^{17}$ esu/g and was independent of the material of the cathode, the gas in the discharge tube, or the velocity of the beam.   It was about 1800 times larger than the $e/m$ found for hydrogen ions in electrolysis,

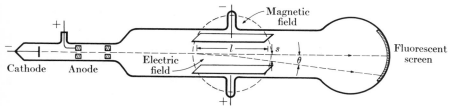

**Fig. 2.1**   *Thomson's apparatus for measuring e/m for cathode rays.*

indicating that the electron had a mass $\frac{1}{1800}$ of that of the hydrogen ion, if the charges were the same.

All experiments utilizing the deflection of charged particles in electric and magnetic fields have one limitation in common: they provide a measure of the ratio $e/m$ but do not give $e$ or $m$ separately.  A different kind of experiment is needed to measure the charge of the electron.  Although the conclusions from Thomson's experiments were hard to refute on any logical grounds, the final proof of the particle nature of electricity and the first precise measurement of the electronic charge came with the results of Millikan's oil-drop experiment in 1909.

Millikan's classic experiment utilized the rate of fall in air of tiny droplets of oil, to which electric charges had been attached by ionizing the air with x-rays.  A charged droplet, when viewed with a microscope, can be accelerated upward or downward or suspended by applying a vertical electrostatic field.  With zero field the drop will fall at a slow uniform rate with its weight balanced by the viscous drag of the surrounding air, from which the size and weight of the droplet can be determined.  With an applied electric field to produce an additional force, the drop will move with a different velocity.  The number of unit electric charges on the droplet can be changed by another pulse of x-rays; in this case the electric force is different and still other velocities are observed.  By using the measured velocities of fall (or rise) and the known values of other fundamental constants (including the viscosity of air), the charge on the droplet can be determined.

Millikan found the values of charge for each droplet studied to be small integral multiples of a unit electron charge $e$.  His first reported value of $e$ was later found to disagree with that obtained from the analysis of spectra using ruled gratings.  The discrepancy was found to be due to use of an erroneous value for the viscosity of air; a more accurate value gave the charge to be $e = q = -(4.803 \pm 0.005) \times 10^{-10}$ esu.*

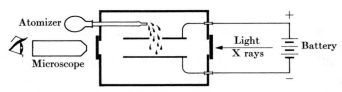

**Fig. 2.2**   *Millikan's oil-drop experiment for measuring the charge of the electron.*

Long before Millikan made his definitive measurement of the unit charge, the particle nature of the electron had been accepted by most scientists.  It became the first elementary particle to be recognized.  It was known to be a constituent of atoms, to be the unit of charge in current electricity, and to be the freely moving charged particle observed in cathode rays and in other electron beams.

It now became evident that the mass of the atom was associated with the positive charge it contained, rather than with the very light electrons.  Although a nuclear atom model, with rings of rotating electrons, had been proposed by Nagaoka as early as 1904, it was discounted on the basis of the classical electromagnetic theory, which required that such orbiting electrons should continually radiate energy because of their central acceleration and rapidly collapse into the central nucleus.  To avoid this difficulty, J. J. Thomson proposed an atomic model in which the electrons were distributed symmetrically within a

* *In particle physics e is used as the symbol of the electron particle and q is the magnitude of its charge or that of any other singly charged particle.*

sphere of positive charge having a uniform density. Although this model was subject to mathematical calculation of its stability and structure, it could not explain the wide variety of atomic phenomena known at that time.

## NATURAL RADIOACTIVITY

The discovery at the turn of the century of natural radioactivity in the heavy elements provided other insights into the structure of the atom. Radioactive atoms were observed to transmute

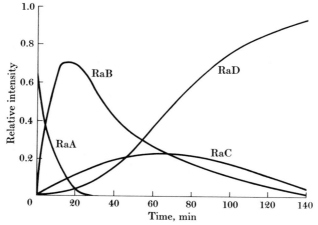

**Fig. 2.3** *Decay of RaA, showing growth and decay of RaB, RaC, and RaD.*

themselves spontaneously into completely different elements, with the emission of $\alpha$ particles, $\beta$ particles, and $\gamma$ rays. The exponential laws which govern the decay and growth of radioactive substances were formulated by Rutherford and Soddy in 1902. Chemical identification of the parent and product elements associated with the different lifetimes established the decay sequences of three radioactive series, originating in thorium, uranium, and actinium. The $\alpha$ particles were identified as positively charged ions of helium; they were emitted in groups having discrete ranges in absorbers and so presumably having discrete energies.   The β particles were found to have a negative charge and to have an *e/m* ratio identical with that of the electron.   The γ rays were observed to be electromagnetic radiations similar to x-rays of the same energy.   Soddy and others estab-

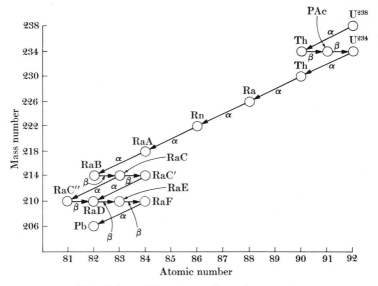

**Fig. 2.4**   *Uranium-radium decay series.*

lished the displacement law: the emission of an α particle results in a product atom which is displaced leftward by two columns in the Mendeleev periodic table, while a β particle causes a displacement of one column to the right.   The obvious interpretation was that atoms are not indivisible entities but are built up out of common and elementary building blocks.

Rutherford recognized that these α particles were unique tools for further studies of atomic structure.   Early measurements of their deflections in magnetic fields showed most groups to have energies of several million electron volts. They could be detected, when observed with a microscope against a dark background, through the scintillations produced when they struck a fluorescent screen.

Studies, first by Rutherford and then by Geiger and Marsden, on the scattering of $\alpha$ particles by air and by thin foils of mica, gold, and other materials, showed that many were deflected through angles greater than 90°. The number of large-angle scatterings was far in excess of that calculated from the uniform-density atomic model proposed by Thomson. Rutherford proposed in 1911 that the positive charge of the atom was concentrated in a very small, central nucleus and showed by calculations that this model could explain the observed large angular deflections of $\alpha$ particles. Atomic dimensions had been established as of the order of $10^{-8}$ cm, which was the size assumed for the Thomson model; the nucleus of the Rutherford model must have a diameter of less than $10^{-12}$ cm.

Once the existence of a small, massive, positive nucleus had been established, with an array of electrons occupying a very much larger volume surrounding the nucleus, it became necessary to question the classical electromagnetic theory which forbade stable electron orbits. The time was ripe for Bohr's postulate of stable, nonradiating orbits and for his successful theory of energy states and energy transitions which explained the origin of atomic spectra (see Chap. 3). The Bohr atom was an elegantly simple concept, introducing some satisfyingly simple—though at that time unusual—postulates concerning the quantization of angular momentum and energy. The scientist's faith in the ultimate simplicity of nature was reaffirmed.

## POSITIVE RAYS AND THE PROTON

Speculations on the structure of the atom go far back into scientific history. As early as 1815, Prout suggested that the primordial substance of all elements are atoms of hydrogen.

This suggestion was based on evidence from chemical analysis and from experiments on electrolysis that the atomic weights of many elements are close to integral multiples of that of hydrogen. When more accurate determinations showed some atomic weights that were not integral multiples, Prout's hypothesis was abandoned, only to be revived again decades later in a new form when the nonintegral atomic weights were explained as isotopes (see page 20).

While Thomson was studying the cathode rays (negative particles) produced in gaseous discharges, Goldstein in 1886 observed that, if the cathode of a discharge tube was pierced with small holes (canals), particles emerged traveling in the opposite direction which, when deflected by magnetic or electric fields, proved to consist of positively charged particles. These were called *canal rays* or *positive rays*. The magnitude of the deflections depended on the type of gas in the discharge. The largest value of $e/m$ observed in these early experiments was that for hydrogen, which was close to the value obtained in electrolysis. These results suggested that positive rays are streams of positive ions produced in the gas by ionization and that in the case of hydrogen gas they are hydrogen ions. It is not clear at what point in this development the positive hydrogen ion was given the name proton, but long before it was isolated and definitive measurements were made of its properties, the proton became an accepted concept.

Thomson measured the $e/m$ values for positive ions in the 1920s. His method was a modification of his earlier experiments on the $e/m$ of electrons, this time using the positive rays from a gaseous discharge which emerge through a channel in the cathode. The beam of positive ions was directed through a region of parallel electric and magnetic fields, transverse to the beam direction, and was observed on a fluorescent screen (or photographic plate) in the evacuated tube. The electric field produces a transverse deflection $y$ in one coordinate [see Eq. (2.2)], and the magnetic field produces a deflection $z$ in the other coordinate. These deflections are projected linearly to the photographic plate where the beam produces an image (see Fig. 2.5).

The deflecting force on a particle of mass $m$ and charge $e$ due to the electric field is $Ee$, and that due to the magnetic field is

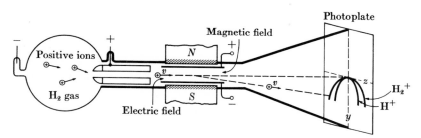

**Fig. 2.5** *Thomson's method of positive-ray analysis, giving parabolic traces for each value of $e/m$.*

$Hev$, where $v$ is particle velocity. The forces act for a time $t = l/v$, where $l$ is the length of the region of fields. Since $F = ma$ and displacement $s = \frac{1}{2}at^2$, the transverse deflections are given by

$$y = \frac{1}{2}\frac{Ee}{m}\left(\frac{l}{v}\right)^2 \tag{2.5}$$

$$\text{and } z = \frac{1}{2}\frac{Hev}{m}\left(\frac{l}{v}\right)^2 \tag{2.6}$$

The relation between the transverse deflections is obtained by eliminating $v$ from these equations; we find

$$z^2 = C\,\frac{e}{m}\frac{H^2}{E}\,y \tag{2.7}$$

where $C$ is a constant depending only on the geometry of the experiment. This is a parabola in the $y$-$z$ plane. A group of positive ions having the same $e/m$ but different velocities will fall on a parabolic curve on the photographic plate. Ions with other values of $e/m$ will form parabolic traces displaced from the first one. By a systematic analysis of the relative positions of the various parabolic traces on a series of plates, for different source gases, Thomson was able to identify and measure the relative $e/m$ values for many ions, such as $H^+$, $H_2^+$, $0^+$, $0_2^+$, $CO^+$, etc.

Hydrogen is of particular interest since it is the lightest of all elements. Its positive ion $H^+$ is the nucleus of the hydrogen atom, with a charge $+e$ (or $+q$). The name *proton* had been assigned to this fundamental constituent of atoms. Although the unique character of the element hydrogen had long been recognized, Thomson's studies of the positive rays from ionized hydrogen gas were the first experiments in which the proton was isolated and identified as a particle. It became the second elementary particle.

Aston extended Thomson's experiments to other gases. When neon was used as the source of ions, two parabolas were observed, one corresponding to the atomic weight ($A$) 20 and a less intense one of atomic weight 22. No element was known of atomic weight 22, but the best value of atomic weight for neon had been determined as 20.20. This average atomic weight results from a mixture of 90 percent of $A^{20}$ and 10 percent of $A^{22}$. This was the first physical evidence for the existence of *isotopes* of the same chemical element with different atomic weights and resolved the problem of fractional atomic weights which had plagued the chemists in their search for order in the periodic table.

The modern instruments used for measuring the $e/m$ values (and so the masses) of positive ions are called *mass spectrographs* and *mass spectrometers*. They are also used for measuring isotope-abundance ratios, for identification of isotopes, and for chemical analysis of gases or vapors. The mass spectrograph is an instrument which disperses the ions of different $e/m$ values and focuses them on a photographic plate as a line spectrum

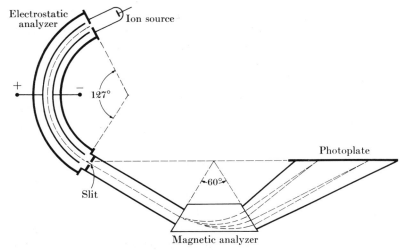

**Fig. 2.6** *Mass spectrograph of Bainbridge and Jordan.*

(see Fig. 2.6). The mass spectrometer brings a focused beam of ions of a specific $e/m$ value through a fixed slit, where it is detected and measured electrically; the analyzing electric and magnetic fields are varied to study the different ions (see Fig. 2.7).

The highest precision is obtained by observing the sepa-

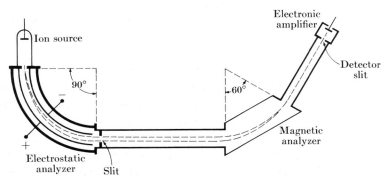

**Fig. 2.7** *Mass spectrometer of Nier and Roberts.*

rations of mass *doublets* of ions having the same integral values of $e/m$ but composed of different ions.   The mass of the hydrogen atom $H^1$ in atomic mass units (see Chap. 5) can be referred to the standard value for $0^{16}$ by using three positive ion doublets: $(H^1{}_2)^+-(H^2)^+$, $(H^2{}_3)^+-(C^{12})^{++}$, and $(C^{12}H^1{}_4)^+-(0^{16})^+$. The observed doublet separations can be written as three simultaneous equations in $H^1$, $H^2$, $C^{12}$, and $0^{16}$, from which solutions are obtained for the three lighter atoms in terms of $0^{16} = 16.0000$ atomic mass units.

The mass differences between positive ions of the light elements known in the 1920s showed a steplike progression up the atomic table in steps very close to the proton mass.   It seemed that nuclei must have integral numbers of protons, but they must also include some electrons to give the net nuclear charge in each case.   For a time it was possible to conceive of a two-particle model of the atom in which the nucleus consists of a closely packed assemblage of protons and electrons, with other electrons in atomic orbits.   The details of this composite nucleus were not clear, but the simplicity of the two-particle atom was appealing.

### NUCLEAR DISINTEGRATION BY $\alpha$ PARTICLES

Rutherford and his colleagues in the Cavendish Laboratory first observed the disintegration of nuclei of light elements by $\alpha$ particles in 1919 as an extension of their work on the scattering of $\alpha$ particles by nuclei.   In measuring the range in gases of $\alpha$ particles from an RaC source, by varying gas pressure in the region between the source and the scintillation screen, they observed that for most gases the scintillations stopped when the gas pressure was equivalent to a range of about 7 cm in air at atmospheric pressure.   However, with nitrogen gas, scintillations continued to pressures equivalent to a range of 40 cm in air.   These long-range particles which produced the scintillations were interpreted by Rutherford to be protons, produced

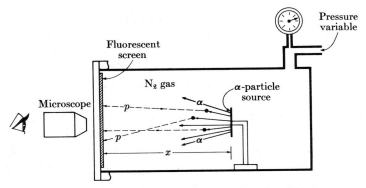

**Fig. 2.8**    *Rutherford's apparatus for observing disintegration of nitrogen nuclei by α particles.*

in a disintegration reaction

$$He^4 + N^{14} \rightarrow O^{17} + H^1 \qquad (2.8)$$

This result came in the same period when Thomson was measuring the $e/m$ of protons from gaseous discharge. It added further evidence that the proton is a constituent of nuclei and one of the fundamental particles. The $O^{17}$ atom which this disintegration reaction predicts is an isotope of the well-known $O^{16}$, with a nucleus having the same number of positive charges but with one higher mass number. This could be an additional proton-electron pair or, as Rutherford suggested in his Bakerian Lecture to the Royal Society in 1920, this could be a neutral heavy particle with a mass approximately that of the proton.

### THE NEUTRON

Many theoretical difficulties arose in attempting to understand how electrons could be constituents of nuclei. It was difficult to relate the necessarily large binding energies of electrons in the nucleus with the extremely small nuclear dimensions. A more fundamental problem came with the introduction of the wave-mechanical concepts of the symmetry properties of particle wave functions and the statistics of the fundamental particles, which are discussed in Chap. 3.   As we shall see, a basic concept is that each particle has an intrinsic spin $s$ which is one-half of the fundamental unit or quantum of angular momentum and which adds vectorially to give the total nuclear angular momentum.   Nuclei with an odd number of protons plus electrons, each with half-integral spin, should result in half-integral nuclear angular momenta.   But spectroscopic evidence, analyzed quantum mechanically, shows that several such nuclei have integral angular momenta.   A neutral particle with spin $\frac{1}{2}$ would resolve both this contradiction and also many other theoretical difficulties.

Experimentally, the identification of a neutral particle was severely handicapped by the limitation that it would not produce ionization in gases as charged particles do and that it would not be deflected by electric or magnetic fields.   During the 1920s, many unsuccessful attempts were made to produce and observe a neutral particle.   The problem remained unsolved until the early work on the disintegration of nuclei by $\alpha$ particles from radioactive substances provided the opportunity and the tools.

Following Rutherford's report of the disintegration of $N^{14}$ by $\alpha$ particles, other experimenters joined in the study of $\alpha$ particle disintegrations of other light elements.   Bothe and Becker (1930) discovered that when boron and beryllium were bombarded with polonium $\alpha$ particles, a highly penetrating radiation was emitted; for a time this was thought to be high-energy $\gamma$ radiation.   Chadwick at the Cavendish Laboratory studied this radiation in more detail; in 1932 he published evidence that it consisted of neutral particles having a mass similar to that of the proton.   The proof came through measurement of the energy of protons ejected from hydrogenous materials by this radiation, which could only be explained if the radiation producing the recoil protons had a mass close to that of the proton. These observations were rapidly confirmed by other workers. So the neutron became the third elementary particle. Chadwick next observed hydrogen ions recoiling from neutrons in a cloud chamber (see Fig. 2.9), and from their ranges he determined the mass of the neutron to be slightly greater than that of the proton.

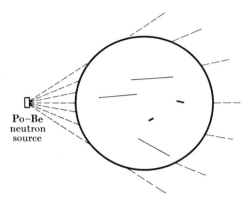

**Fig. 2.9**   *Illustration of cloud-chamber photograph of recoil ions from neutrons. The long tracks are protons from water vapor, and the short, dense tracks are $N^{14}$ ions.*

The nucleus could now be conceived as a closely packed assemblage of protons and neutrons, with the atomic charge number $Z$ given by the number of protons and the atomic weight number $A$ by the total of protons and neutrons. This attractively simple model of a three-particle atom, with a layered cloud of electrons outside the nucleus, seemed to answer all outstanding questions. The three-particle atom provided a model compatible with Bohr's atomic theory, which correlated atomic structure with the quantum theory of radiation as developed by Planck and Einstein, and accounted for many of the properties of atomic structure. It seemed that it was only necessary to fill in the details of the structure of the nucleus. Nature was indeed justifying the scientists' faith in the concept that all atoms are formed of a few elementary particles.

### STRONG NUCLEAR FORCE

An atomic nucleus composed of protons and neutrons can be stable only if there is a strongly attractive force between these particles. The electrostatic force between the charged protons is repulsive and would tend to blow the nucleus apart unless it were held together by some specifically nuclear force. The need for such a nuclear force was indicated by the conclusions from Rutherford's scattering experiments, which showed that the nucleus had such small dimensions, and from his disintegration experiments, which indicated the extremely high energies required to transmute one stable nucleus into another. However, experimental evidence on the nature and strength of this force was not obtained until a much later date.

Some direct evidence came from studies of the elastic scattering of protons by protons when particle accelerators were developed to produce the high-energy beams required. At relatively low bombarding energies, where the "closest distance of approach" calculated from the coulomb force between the electric charges is greater than about $10^{-12}$ cm, the observed angular distributions in the elastic scattering were found to agree with those calculable from the coulomb force, which varies inversely with the square of the distance of separation. The *coupling constant* used in such calculations is $2\pi e^2/hc \simeq \frac{1}{137}$; this quantity is also known in atomic physics as the *fine structure constant* and is discussed further in Chap. 3.

At higher proton energies, which correspond to smaller values of the minimum separation, the shapes of the angular distributions of the scattered protons change sharply, indicating the onset of another type of force which is attractive and which varies much more rapidly with distance. This nuclear force is equivalent to the coulomb force at a range (half the separation) of about $1.3 \times 10^{-13}$ cm. This distance has been used as one definition of the radius of the proton. The nuclear coupling constant required to describe the magnitude of the attractive force at this distance is about 100 times larger than the coupling constant in the electromagnetic interaction.

Studies of the scattering of protons by neutrons and of neutrons by neutrons show the same magnitude of the nuclear force constant for the same separations. This strong nuclear force is independent of the charge on the particles. It applies to their specifically nuclear character rather than to their charge, and the two particles are identical in this respect. This equivalence has led to use of the term *nucleon* to describe both the proton and the neutron. The nuclear force cannot readily be described as a function of distance. If two nucleons are "touching" they are strongly attracted, but if they are separated by even a few nucleon diameters the force is essentially zero. Other properties of this strong nuclear force will be discussed in chapters to follow.

*chapter 3*

# QUANTA
# AND WAVES
# IN ATOMS

THE IDENTIFICATION OF THE CONSTITUENTS of atoms was only a part of the much larger problem of developing a satisfactory atomic theory. This development has paralleled the experimental discoveries and the study of particle properties, and has benefited in a fundamental way from the theoretical progress in wave mechanics and quantum mechanics. The era started in 1913 with Bohr's quantum theory of the energy states of electrons in atoms and continued through the 1930s with intensive applications of quantum-mechanical theory to atomic problems. By 1940 essentially all of the major new ideas had been introduced and assimilated into the theory. In this chapter we will survey this era and describe the concepts which led to the modern theory of the atom. We start with a statement of the first big problem—the interpretation of the regularities, and also the complexities, observed by spectroscopic study of atomic spectra.

## ATOMIC SPECTRA

When an electric discharge is passed through a gas or vapor from a volatile salt and the light is dispersed by a prism or a grating spectrometer, a spectrum of sharp lines of discrete wavelengths called atomic spectra is observed. Early observations were in the visible region of the spectrum. It was soon found that the spectra extended into the ultraviolet and the infrared regions as well.

The spectrum of atomic hydrogen is of particular interest since it is the lightest and simplest of the elements. The visible spectrum consists of lines with an apparent regularity of spacing, becoming closer together with decreasing wavelength until the limit of the series is reached at 3646 Å (Ångstrom units) (see Fig. 3.1). Balmer first noted this regularity in 1885 and expressed his observations on the nine lines then known in the visible spectrum of hydrogen with a relatively simple formula for the wavelengths. Rydberg, a few years later, found an even sim-

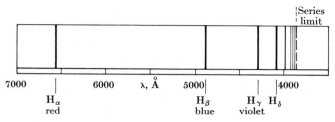

**Fig. 3.1**  *Visible spectrum of ionized hydrogen.*

pler relation in terms of the wave number (reciprocal of the wavelength)

$$\bar{\nu} = \frac{1}{\lambda} = R_H \left( \frac{1}{2^2} - \frac{1}{n^2} \right) \tag{3.1}$$

where $R_H$ is the Rydberg constant for hydrogen, $n$ is a series of integers 3, 4, 5, . . . , and the series limit is for $n = \infty$. The value of $R_H$ has since been determined to high precision through spectroscopic measurements to be $R_H = 109{,}677.576$ cm$^{-1}$.

The hydrogen spectrum was found to contain four other series, one in the ultraviolet and three in the infrared, which are given by simple modifications of the Rydberg formula. Wave numbers for the five hydrogen series are given by

$$\bar{\nu} = R_H \left( \frac{1}{1^2} - \frac{1}{n^2} \right), \, n = 2, \, 3, \, 4, \, . \, . \, . \text{ Lyman series,} \\ \text{ultraviolet}$$

$$\bar{\nu} = R_H \left( \frac{1}{2^2} - \frac{1}{n^2} \right), \, n = 3, \, 4, \, 5, \, . \, . \, . \text{ Balmer series,} \\ \text{visible}$$

$$\bar{\nu} = R_H \left( \frac{1}{3^2} - \frac{1}{n^2} \right), \, n = 4, \, 5, \, 6, \, . \, . \, . \text{ Paschen series,} \\ \text{infrared} \quad (3.2)$$

$$\bar{\nu} = R_H \left( \frac{1}{4^2} - \frac{1}{n^2} \right), \, n = 5, \, 6, \, 7, \, . \, . \, . \text{ Brackett series,} \\ \text{infrared}$$

$$\bar{\nu} = R_H \left( \frac{1}{5^2} - \frac{1}{n^2} \right), \, n = 6, \, 7, \, 8, \, . \, . \, . \text{ Pfund series,} \\ \text{infrared}$$

In complex atoms with many electrons, the spectra consist of many more lines than for hydrogen, representing several overlapping series. Many of these series were identified and expressed in formulas similar to the Rydberg relation for hydrogen, involving the difference between two terms each of which involved integral numbers. In 1908 Ritz extended the Rydberg formulation to include heavier atoms and expressed his general *combination principle*, which states that the wave number of each spectral line of an atomic spectrum can be given, with certain limitations, by the difference between two numerical terms. The clarification of the meaning of these terms became a major theoretical problem. The time was ripe for Bohr's concept of transitions from one energy state to another of lower energy.

The field of atomic spectra is one of the great branches of physics. On the experimental side, instruments have been developed to extend the range of spectra far into the infrared and ultraviolet regions, with high resolution sufficient to observe the splitting of individual lines into their substructures of multiplets. Theoretical progress starting with the Bohr theory has kept pace with experimental information. The observed regularities and the complexities have been "explained" one by one as the theory has been developed. By 1940 spectroscopists had identified a large fraction of the observed spectral lines with the specific initial and final energy states of the atoms concerned.

## THE BOHR ATOM

The Bohr theory of the atom, which first correlated and explained the experimental observations on atomic spectra, is based on the following postulates:

(1)    Atoms exist in a number of "stationary" energy states from which no radiation is emitted, even though the particles may be in relative motion; this differs from the requirement of classical electrodynamics that accelerated charges radiate energy.

(2)    An atomic transition from one energy state to another involves the emission or absorption of radiation of frequency $\nu$ determined by the quantum relation $h\nu = W_1 - W_2$, where $h$ is Planck's constant and $W_1$ and $W_2$ are the energies of the two stationary states.

(3)    In each stationary state the dynamic equilibrium is governed by the laws of classical mechanics including the conservation of energy and momentum.

(4)    The allowed stationary states for a system of one electron revolving about a positively charged nucleus are circular orbits for which the angular momentum is quantized in units of $h/2\pi$.

To illustrate, consider an atom with a single orbiting electron and a nuclear charge $Ze$, where $Z$ is the atomic number.   If $Z = 1$ the atom is neutral hydrogen; if $Z = 2$ it is singly ionized helium, etc.   The angular momentum of the electron in a circular orbit is $mvr$, where $m$ is electron mass, $v$ is its linear velocity, and $r$ is orbit radius.   The fourth Bohr postulate can be expressed as

$$mvr = \frac{nh}{2\pi} \qquad n = 1, 2, 3, \ldots \tag{3.3}$$

Successive circular orbits are determined by the value of $n$, which is called the *principal quantum number.*

Classically, the centripetal force in circular motion is provided by the attractive electrostatic force

$$\frac{mv^2}{r} = \frac{Ze^2}{r^2} \tag{3.4}$$

Solving Eqs. (3.3) and (3.4) for the radius or the velocity

$$r = \frac{n^2h^2}{4\pi^2me^2Z} \tag{3.5}$$

$$v = \frac{2\pi e^2Z}{nh} \tag{3.6}$$

The radii of the allowed orbits are proportional to $n^2$ $(1, 4, 9, \ldots)$. For hydrogen with $Z = 1$, and inserting known values of $m$, $e$, and $h$, we find, for the smallest orbit with $n = 1$, $r_1 = 5.29 \times 10^{-9}$ cm. This is in excellent agreement with estimates of atomic radii obtained by other methods. The relative dimensions of the first five orbits are illustrated in Fig. 3.2. The velocity in the smallest

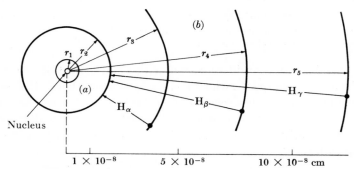

**Fig. 3.2** (a) *Radial dimensions of the first five Bohr orbits in the hydrogen atom, cm.* (b) *Transitions leading to emission of the Balmer spectral lines $H_\alpha$, $H_\beta$, $H_\gamma$.*

orbit is found to be $v_1 = 2.2 \times 10^8$ cm/sec; this is small compared with the velocity of light; so relativistic corrections are negligible and $m$ can be taken as the rest mass of the electron.

The kinetic energy of the electron is

$$T = \tfrac{1}{2}mv^2 = \frac{1}{2}\frac{Ze^2}{r} \qquad (3.7)$$

The electrostatic potential energy is negative (using the accepted convention that it is zero at infinite separation) and is given by

$$U = -\frac{Ze^2}{r} \qquad (3.8)$$

The total mechanical energy, $W = T + U$, of a stationary state of quantum number $n$ is also negative and given by

$$W_n = -\frac{1}{2}\frac{Ze^2}{r} = -\frac{2\pi^2 m e^4 Z^2}{n^2 h^2} \qquad (3.9)$$

Following the second Bohr postulate, the frequency of the quantum of radiation emitted by a transition from state $W_2$ to $W_1$ is

$$\nu = \frac{W_1 - W_2}{h} = \frac{2\pi^2 m e^4}{h^3} Z^2 \left( \frac{1}{n_2{}^2} - \frac{1}{n_1{}^2} \right) \tag{3.10a}$$

Expressed in wave numbers

$$\bar{\nu} = \frac{\nu}{c} = R_\infty Z^2 \left( \frac{1}{n_2{}^2} - \frac{1}{n_1{}^2} \right) \tag{3.10b}$$

where

$$R_\infty = \frac{2\pi^2 m e^4}{c h^3}$$

The equation above has exactly the same form (for $Z = 1$) as the empirical Rydberg relation, Eq. (3.1), for the lines of the Balmer series in hydrogen. The importance of the Bohr theory is that it gives a value of the experimentally determined constant $R$ in terms of the fundamental constants and allows a direct numerical comparison of theory with experiment. It also identifies the sequence of integers in the Rydberg relation with the quantum numbers postulated by Bohr to define the allowed energy states in the atomic system.

Before proceeding with the comparison, it is necessary to correct for an approximation used so far that the electron moves in a circular orbit with the nucleus fixed at the center as though it were of infinite mass. In hydrogen the nucleus has a mass 1836 times that of the electron; both the electron and the nucleus revolve about their common center of mass. The effect of this motion on the total angular momentum is to replace the mass $m$ of the electron by a reduced mass $mM/(m + M)$, where $M$ is the mass of the nucleus. The relation between the Rydberg constant for a fixed nucleus, $R_\infty$, and the Rydberg constant for hydrogen is

$$R_H = R_\infty \frac{1}{1 + (m/M_H)} = 0.9994 R_\infty \qquad (3.11)$$

When this correction is applied, the theoretical value of the Rydberg constant for hydrogen is $R_H$ (theor.) = 109,681 cm$^{-1}$. This can be compared with the best experimental value $R_H$ (expt.) = 109,677.576 cm$^{-1}$. The agreement is within the uncertainty in the best values of the fundamental constants and represents a major triumph for the Bohr theory.

The Bohr theory provides a physical interpretation of the origin of atomic radiation. Spectral lines come from transitions of the atomic electrons from one stationary energy state to another of lower total energy. The lowest state is described by the principal quantum number $n = 1$ and is called the *ground state*. The electron can also reside, temporarily, in one or another of the higher energy, or excited, states. In a large sample of the element, when it is excited by some mechanism for removing electrons from the ground state such as by electric discharge, all allowed energy states will be occupied by some of the atoms. Transitions from higher to lower energy states result in the several series of emission lines. Transitions leading to the Balmer series lines H$_\alpha$, H$_\beta$, and H$_\gamma$ are illustrated in Fig. 3.2.

Absorption lines represent transitions from the ground state to one or another of the excited states, when the amount of energy available is precisely that required to accomplish the excitation. This excitation energy can be provided by a photon of the exact frequency of the emission line, by electron impact with electrons of sufficient kinetic energy, or by several other mechanisms.

The stationary states or energy terms of the atom can be represented graphically as an energy-level diagram. Figure 3.3 is the energy-level diagram of the hydrogen atom, with increasing negative values of total energy $W$ below a zero energy assigned to the ionized atom for which $n = \infty$. On this scale, the ground state has an energy of $-13.597$ eV, the energy required to remove a ground-state electron completely from the atom, that is, to ionize the atom. Free electrons attaching to such an ionized atom can be captured temporarily in any one of the allowed energy levels, emitting a quantum of radiation. An excited atom, in which an electron is in some state other than the ground state, can have a transition to a lower state. In Fig. 3.3 the

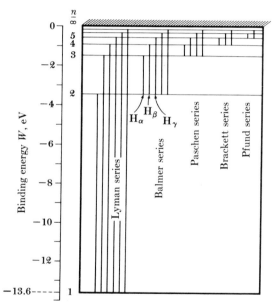

**Fig. 3.3** *Energy-level diagram of the hydrogen atom.*

several series of emission lines from hydrogen [Eq. (3.2)] are plotted as vertical lines between energy states, with lengths proportional to the frequency or energy of the photons emitted in the transition. The quantum numbers $n$, which define the number of $h/2\pi$ units of angular momentum, form an ascending set of rungs on the ladder of allowed energy states.

The simple Bohr theory has been extended by later workers to describe additional complexities in the observed spectra. Many spectral lines were observed to have a fine structure, consisting of a number of component lines lying close together. To explain this fine structure, Sommerfeld postulated the existence of elliptical as well as circular orbits, with radial momentum in addition to angular momentum. In both degrees of freedom the momentum is quantized in units of $h/2\pi$. The principal quantum number has two components, an orbital (or azimuthal) quantum number $l$ and a radial quantum number $n_r$, such that the sum $l + n_r = n$. For any value of $n$ greater than unity, the orbits can be ellipses with discrete eccentricities (see Fig. 3.4).

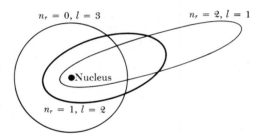

**Fig. 3.4** *Quantized elliptical orbits for $n = 3$.*

For such elliptical orbits a relativistic correction to the energy is required to represent the variation of mass with velocity; this results in small energy differences between orbits of different eccentricity and in the transition energies between states, leading to the observed fine structure. The mathematical analysis is quite complicated and need not be given here. In the Sommerfeld formula the energy terms involve the quantum numbers $n$ and $l$, and the magnitude of the energy differences is given by a quantity called the *fine structure constant*, $\alpha = 2\pi e^2/hc = \frac{1}{137}$. The early Sommerfeld theory predicted more spectral-line components than were observed experimentally. Agreement was obtained by introducing a limitation, called a selection rule, in which only those transitions are allowed for which $\Delta l = \pm 1$. The spectra of single-electron atoms such as $He^+$ and $Li^{++}$ are also explained by the Bohr theory, where the energies of the corresponding stationary states are larger by the factor $Z^2$. However, for two-electron atoms such as neutral He and $Li^+$, there were serious discrepancies between the Bohr theory predictions and experimental observations. Spectral lines from multielectron atoms were found to be split into multiplets (doublets, triplets, etc.) with spacings large compared with the fine-structure splitting, which could not be explained with the two quantum numbers $n$ and $l$. A well-known example is the sodium D-line doublet which gives the yellow color to the light from a sodium-vapor lamp. Multiplet structure was also observed in many cases when the light source was placed in a magnetic field. To describe these observations a third "magnetic" quantum number $m$ was introduced. In the presence of a magnetic field, either externally applied or caused by the orbital motions of other electrons, electron orbits are distorted so that a three-dimensional or spatial quantization is necessary. The magnetic quantum number $m$ can be visualized as applying to the angular-momentum component along the $z$ coordinate relative to the plane of the elliptical orbit. This component is also quantized in units of $h/2\pi$ and is assigned zero or integral values. With this third quantum number many of the observations described above could be explained. But, again, observations showed fewer transitions than allowed by the early theory and required the selection rule $\Delta m = 0$ or $\pm 1$.

When the principles of the wave mechanics (see pages **47** *et seq.*) were applied to atomic structure, the classical picture of electrons revolving in planetary orbits about the nucleus was no longer essential as a model for calculations. The three quantum numbers $n$, $l$, and $m$ appear in a direct way in the mathematical theory of the two-electron atom and the necessary selection rules also follow as a direct result of the mathematical treatment.

The quantum mechanical theory yields all the successful results of the Bohr theory and solves many problems which the Bohr theory could not handle.

Quantum mechanics introduced a fourth, and final, quantum number to represent the angular momentum of the electron spinning about its own axis.   An electron spin $s$ was proposed by Uhlenbeck and Goudsmit in 1926 to account for the observed multiplet structure of spectra and other phenomena such as the "anomalous" Zeeman effect.   Spin is a vector with only two allowed orientations, parallel or antiparallel to the orbital angular momentum vector.   The magnitude of the electron spin is half the $h/2\pi$ unit of angular momentum.   As a quantum number, $s$ can have only the two values $+\frac{1}{2}$ and $-\frac{1}{2}$, representing the two allowed orientations.

A fundamental rule in quantum mechanics is the *Pauli exclusion principle*, which determines the quantum numbers which an atomic electron can have.   The exclusion principle states that no two electrons in an atom can have the same four quantum numbers $n$, $l$, $m$, and $s$.   This leads to shells of electrons for each value of the principle quantum number $n$, with $2n^2$ electrons in each shell.   In any atom the electrons occupy the lowest energy states first, with two electrons in the $n = 1$ shell, 8 in the $n = 2$ shell, 18 in the $n = 3$ shell, etc.   The form of the periodic table of the elements can be completely accounted for by this shell structure of electrons and the number of electrons "outside" the last closed shell (the "valence" electrons).

### LIGHT: WAVES OR PARTICLES?

The nature of light has been a mystery for centuries.   It was known in the eighteenth century that light traveled with a very large but finite speed, that it moved in straight lines, and that it carried energy.   White light was known to consist of a mixture of colors which could be refracted and separated by prisms.   The fundamental question was whether light was a wave motion or a stream of particles.   The argument lasted for over one hundred years, and both theories had their supporters. Newton is believed to have favored the particle theory. Huygens and Fresnel found convincing evidence for the wave theory through studies of the phenomena of diffraction and interference, which also provided techniques for measuring the wavelengths of light. The most convincing evidence came with Maxwell's theory of the electromagnetic field, which introduced the concept of displacement currents in a hypothetical ether which pervaded all space and was the medium for transmitting transverse electric and magnetic waves. The triumph of the Maxwell theory was that it predicted quantitatively the observed velocity of light. By 1900 it seemed certain that light was an electromagnetic wave phenomenon, although the mechanical concept of an ether to support transverse vibrations was unsatisfying.

The discovery of the quantum principle by Planck in 1899, followed by a sequence of applications, brought new evidence for the particle nature of light. Planck found that the observed distribution in energy in the spectrum of radiation from a heated body could best be explained if the emission and absorption of radiation occurs in bundles of definite size (quanta) proportional to the frequency of the light. Einstein used this concept in 1905 to provide a quantum theory of the photoelectric effect. It was known that electrons emitted from the surface of certain metals when exposed to ultraviolet light were emitted with energies which were determined not by the light intensity but by its color. Einstein assumed that each *photon* consists of a packet of energy, $E = h\nu$, where $\nu$ is the frequency and $h$ is a fundamental constant of proportionality called the Planck constant.* He proposed that each photon could extract one electron, requiring an amount of work characteristic of the surface (the work function $W$), with the remainder as kinetic energy. The energy of the electron as measured by a stopping potential $V$ is given by

$$Ve = \tfrac{1}{2}mv^2 = h\nu - W \tag{3.12}$$

---

\* $h = 0.66 \times 10^{-27} eV$ sec.

The number of electrons is proportional to light intensity, but their energy depends on the frequency of the light (see Fig. 3.5). Experimental work by Millikan and others (see Fig. 3.5) soon confirmed the validity of this theory and firmly established the

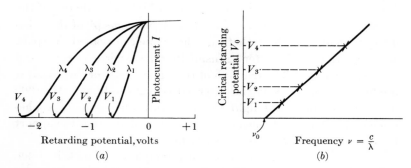

Fig. 3.5   *The photoelectric effect. (a) Retarding potentials for different wavelengths of light. (b) Plot of critical-retarding potential versus frequency to determine the work function of the surface,* $W = h\nu_0$.

particle nature of light. Einstein's concept that $E = h\nu$ for photons was an essential feature of Bohr's theory of the atom.

It is now recognized that light has both wave and particle properties; this duality in its nature is accepted as a basic fact of nature. The photon is believed to be the mediating agency of the electromagnetic force; it provides the mechanism for transferring energy between electric charges; it is the "stuff" of the electromagnetic field. But photons of discrete energies are also released (as γ rays) from nuclear decays and particle interactions. So the photon is generally listed as a special type of elementary particle, with zero mass and zero charge. Its special character is that it is involved only in electromagnetic interactions, that it obeys the *Bose-Einstein* statistics (see page 58), and that it has an intrinsic spin of 1 (in which it differs from all other elementary particles).

## RELATIVISTIC CONCEPTS

Another development during those fruitful years when atomic theory was being formulated was Einstein's special theory of relativity. The concepts of special relativity became essential components in the atomic theory and provided the small corrections which brought atomic theory into precise agreement with experiment. They have also had a tremendous impact on other sciences, such as astronomy and astrophysics, and on philosophic thought. Although this survey is not the place for a detailed presentation, these basic concepts and conclusions are now part of our scientific heritage and deserve to be presented.

Classical kinematics is the analysis of the motions and interactions of particles (and extended objects) at velocities small relative to that of light, based on the equations of motion which follow from the laws of conservation of energy and momentum, which are discussed in Chap. 5. The usual coordinate system is in the laboratory frame of reference.

In describing systems in which velocities approach that of light, special relativity requires that the classical kinematics be abandoned. A basic assumption is that no velocity can exceed the velocity of light $c$. Interactions involving particle velocities approaching that of light in the laboratory frame of reference can also be described in a frame of reference located on the moving particle, or a coordinate system can be chosen in which the center of mass (CM) of the interacting particles is at rest. Such coordinate systems have velocities relative to each other. The ratio of the relative velocity to that of light, $v/c$, as judged by an observer in one system, becomes a measure of the deviations of relativistic kinematics from classical kinematics. See Fig. 3.6.

If one moving system has "proper" coordinates $x$, $y$, and $z$ and "proper" time $t$, and another system which is observed to be moving with velocity $v$ relative to the first (taken for convenience in the $x$ direction) has the coordinates $x'$, $y'$, and $z'$ and time $t'$, the coordinates of the two systems are related through the *Lorentz*

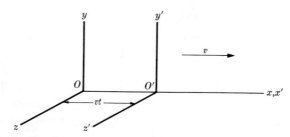

**Fig. 3.6** *Two frames of reference with relative velocity* **v.**

*transformations:*

$$x' = \frac{x - vt}{(1 - v^2/c^2)^{\frac{1}{2}}}$$

$$y' = y$$

$$z' = z \qquad\qquad (3.13)$$

$$t' = \frac{t - vx/c^2}{(1 - v^2/c^2)^{\frac{1}{2}}}$$

These relations for $x'$ and $t'$ can be solved to give

$$x'^2 - c^2t'^2 = x^2 - c^2t^2 \qquad\qquad (3.14)$$

The Lorentz formulation implies a four-dimensional space with the coordinates $x$, $y$, $z$, and $ict$ (where $i = \sqrt{-1}$), in which the square of the distance from the origin is given by $x^2 + y^2 + z^2 - (ict)^2$. From Eq. (3.14), it is evident that if $x = ct$, then $x' = ct'$, or that the velocity of light is independent of the motion of the observer. There is no fixed "ether" in which light is propagated. The basic ideas of mechanics must be altered in such a way that a body having finite mass can never be accelerated up to the velocity of light.

Further, we see that the distance between two points in one system is related to that in the other system, as

$$x_1 - x_2 = (x'_1 - x'_2)(1 - v^2/c^2)^{\frac{1}{2}} \qquad (3.15)$$

Hence, lengths in the moving system appear to an observer in the first system to be contracted by the relativistic term $(1 - v^2/c^2)^{\frac{1}{2}}$. So dimensions are relative, depending on the system in which the measurements are made. The time separating two events in one system is related to that in the other system, as

$$t_1' - t_2' = \frac{(t_1 - t_2)}{(1 - v^2/c^2)^{\frac{1}{2}}} \qquad (3.16)$$

So the time between two events in the second system, observed from the first system, is longer or is "dilated."

The momentum of a moving particle can be defined by its mass $m$ and its velocity components $dx/dt$, etc., in one system, or by $dx'/dt'$, etc., in the other system. If $m_0$ is the mass in the primed system (in which the particle is at rest), we have for the other system

$$m \frac{dx}{dt} = \frac{m_0}{(1 - v^2/c^2)^{\frac{1}{2}}} \frac{dx}{dt} \qquad (3.17)$$

where $m_0$ is the *rest mass* and $v$ is the velocity of the particle in the system in which the measurements are made. The mass is given by the formula

$$m = \frac{m_0}{(1 - v^2/c^2)^{\frac{1}{2}}} \qquad (3.18)$$

The energy is given by

$$E = mc^2 = \frac{m_0 c^2}{(1 - v^2/c^2)^{\frac{1}{2}}} \qquad (3.19)$$

and the momentum is

$$p = mv = \frac{m_0 v}{(1 - v^2/c^2)^{\frac{1}{2}}} \qquad (3.20)$$

From these latter two expressions we find the relation between $m_0$, $E$, and $p$ which is basic in the analysis of relativistic mechanics

$$m_0 = \frac{1}{c^2} (E^2 - p^2 c^2)^{\frac{1}{2}} \qquad (3.21)$$

For the special case where $m_0$ is zero, such as for photons or zero-mass particles, the energy and the momentum are related as

$$E = pc \qquad (3.22)$$

The inertial mass associated with a photon or a zero-mass particle is

$$m = \frac{p}{c} = \frac{E}{c^2} \qquad (3.23)$$

Einstein predicted that gravitation would affect inertial mass exactly as it affects the gravitational (or rest) mass. This was confirmed through astronomical observations of the lateral displacement of the images of stars beyond the sun during an eclipse, when their light ($m = h\nu/c^2$) was deflected by the gravitational field of the sun. The variation of mass with velocity given by the equations above has also been verified in many precise numerical correlations in spectroscopy between the theoretical predictions based on the quantized momenta in elliptical orbits and the observed energy differences in the fine structure of spectral lines. In particle accelerators the total mass of the accelerated particles is observed to increase with their increasing energy, in agreement with the equations above.

## CONCEPTS OF WAVE MECHANICS

The growing understanding of the wave-particle dualism in the properties of light led Louis de Broglie in 1925 to propound the hypothesis that a material particle should also have a wave property associated with it. The frequency of the associated particle wave should be related to the total particle energy by the relation $E = h\nu$, just as it is for the photon. Furthermore, the wavelength must have the same relationship as for light waves, in which the momentum $p = h/\lambda$.

This hypothesis had a built-in "irrationality," as Bohr called it, in attempting to correlate the divergent concepts of point-mass particles and of wave motion. In classical mechanics the concepts of energy and momentum have been associated with particles of negligibly small dimensions; waves were considered to be infinitely extended in space and in time. The great success of the wave mechanics, as applied to the quantum theory of matter, was in combining these divergent concepts into a consistent whole.

Meanwhile, unexplained experimental phenomena on the behavior of electrons had been accumulating. Metals showed abnormal values of specific heat, which was thought to be associated with the behavior of the free electrons in the metal. Studies of the scattering of beams of electrons by metallic targets in vacuum showed more electrons deflected at certain angles than at others. Elsasser in 1925 conjectured that this effect might be due to a diffraction of electron waves by the lattices of metallic crystals, similar to the known diffraction effects of x-rays. Davisson and Germer in 1927 treated metallic targets to enhance their crystal structure and obtained electron diffraction patterns quite similar to the Laue patterns observed with x-rays which are diffracted in crystals. Thus, the wave character of electrons was experimentally established independent of the theoretical proposals of de Broglie.

The correlation of the experimental results with the theory

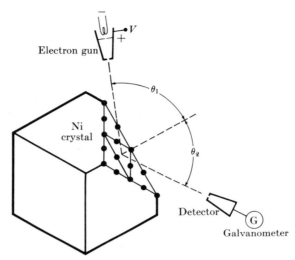

**Fig. 3.7** *Schematic arrangement for observing scattering of electron waves from the lattice of a nickel crystal.*

of matter waves can be illustrated with a numerical example. The velocity of electrons in a cathode-ray tube is determined by the applied accelerating potential $V$ through the relation $\frac{1}{2}mv^2 = Ve$. For low velocities where relativistic corrections are not required, the wavelength given by de Broglie's relation is

$$\lambda = \frac{h}{mv} = \frac{h}{(2meV)^{\frac{1}{2}}} = \frac{1.22}{V^{\frac{1}{2}}} \times 10^{-7} \text{ cm} \qquad (3.24)$$

where $V$ is in volts. With an accelerating potential of 10,000 volts, which is typical of the values used by Davisson and Germer, the wavelength of the electrons would be

$$\lambda = 1.22 \times 10^{-9} \text{ cm} = 0.122 \text{ Å}$$

This is in the region of the spectrum of hard x-rays. The lattice spacings for metallic crystals have dimensions of about

$10^{-8}$ cm or 1 Å. Assuming that the electron diffraction patterns came from lattice planes in the metallic crystals having this spacing, the wavelengths could be calculated. Detailed analysis of Davisson and Germer's results gave striking correlations with the de Broglie wavelengths.

Further experiments with electron beams showed other types of interference phenomena and fully justified their wave nature. Electron diffraction is now used as an analytical technique for research on crystal structure in metals and in many other fields. The electron microscope has become one of our most valuable scientific instruments; beams of electrons can be accelerated to high energies for which their short wavelengths [from Eq. (3.24)] give much higher resolution than that of optical instruments, and the beams can be sharply focused with electric and magnetic fields.

According to de Broglie, the frequency of matter waves is given by the particle energy, $\nu = E/h$, while the wavelength is given by its momentum, $\lambda = h/mv$. The velocity associated with the frequency and wavelength is the *phase* or *wave* velocity, $w = \nu\lambda$. This is the velocity with which a particular phase of the wave moves through space. Consider a pulse of water waves originating from the point where a stone strikes the water, and focus attention on a particular wave crest. The crest moves through the wave and dies out as it reaches the trailing edge of the train; as it does, new waves appear at the front of the train. The velocity with which the general disturbance moves is the *group* velocity; the velocity of the wave crest relative to the water is the *phase* velocity.

Conceptually, a wave train of finite length may be regarded as a superposition of a large number of (sinusoidal) waves of slightly different wavelengths. Each component will move with a slightly different velocity. Through constructive interference, there will be an amplitude maximum or "hump"; the velocity with which this hump moves is the group velocity, and this velocity determines the rate of energy flow or transfer in the wave motion. The phase velocity, which depends on the fre-

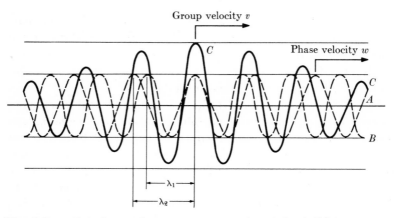

**Fig. 3.8**   *Interference between two waves A and B of different wavelengths $\lambda_1$ and $\lambda_2$ moving with phase velocity w, resulting in an amplitude maximum C moving with group velocity v.*

quency and wavelength, determines the phase of the wave motion. In general, these two velocities differ. However, it can be shown (by Fermat's principle of least time) that their product is a constant. In the special case of matter waves, for a free particle moving with velocity $v$, with wavelength $\lambda = h/mv$, and with frequency $\nu = E/h$, the group velocity $v$ is exactly the particle velocity and is related to the phase velocity as

$$v = \frac{c^2}{w} \qquad\qquad (3.25)$$

The particle can now be visualized as a *wave packet* centered on the amplitude maximum due to superposition of a number of wave trains and moving with the velocity $v$ (see Fig. 3.9). This interpretation has difficulties, since a wave packet of this kind is not a stable mechanical system and dissipates rapidly. However, it does provide a theoretical formulation for the description of the wave properties of matter, developed by Schrödinger in the form of his *wave equation*.

The Schrödinger wave equation is based on the well-known differential equation for a traveling wave in a homogeneous medium

$$\frac{\partial^2 \Psi}{\partial x_2} = \frac{1}{w^2} \frac{\partial^2 \Psi}{\partial t^2} \qquad (3.26)$$

where $\Psi$ is the amplitude, $w$ is the phase velocity, and $x$ is the distance in the direction of propagation. For a plane wave in an isotropic medium, the solutions are harmonic functions of the form

$$\Psi = A \frac{\sin}{\cos} 2\pi \left( \nu t \pm \frac{x}{\lambda} \right) \qquad (3.27)$$

The frequency $\nu$ and the wavelength $\lambda$ are determined by the properties of the medium. The quantity $(\nu t - x/\lambda)$ is a constant on a moving surface of constant phase; by differentiation we obtain $dx/dt = w = \nu\lambda$, where $w$ is the phase velocity. When suitable boundary conditions are imposed the solutions become standing waves, such as those in stretched strings or in organ pipes.

Another solution of Eq. (3.26), which separates the variables, is

$$\Psi = \psi(x) e^{-2\pi i \nu t} \qquad (3.28)$$

in which $\psi(x)$ is a function of position only and describes the "shape" of the wave at some instant in time. $\psi(x)$ is called the *wave function*. When this is substituted in the wave equation we obtain

$$\frac{\partial^2}{\partial x^2} \psi(x) + \left( \frac{2\pi}{\lambda} \right)^2 \psi(x) = 0 \qquad (3.29)$$

For a particle of mass $m$ and momentum $p$, which has kinetic energy $p^2/2m$, potential energy $U$, and total energy

$$W = \frac{p^2}{2m} + U$$

the wavelength $\lambda$ is given by the de Broglie relation [Eq. (3.24)] to be

$$\lambda = \frac{h}{p} = \frac{h}{[2m(W - U)]^{\frac{1}{2}}} \qquad (3.30)$$

For such a particle, a commonly used form of Schrödinger's equation, in one dimension, is

$$\frac{\partial^2 \psi(x)}{\partial x^2} + \frac{8\pi^2 m(W - U)}{h^2} \psi(x) = 0 \qquad (3.31)$$

where $\psi(x)$ is the spatial wave function, or the shape of the wave packet, for the particle.

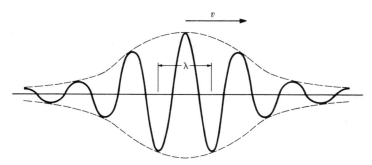

**Fig. 3.9**   *Visualization of particle wave packet of wavelength $\lambda$ moving with velocity v.*

Another, and somewhat more satisfactory, interpretation or visualization of the wave properties of material particles, proposed by Born, is based on the concept of probability.   The Schrödinger wave equation describes a wave packet in which the amplitude varies in space and time.   The square of the amplitude (the product of $\Psi$ and its complex conjugate $\Psi^*$ in which $i$ is replaced by $-i$ in the wave function) describes the probability that the particle is at a particular location at a specific instant in time. In the scattering of one particle by another, each is conceived as having an associated de Broglie wavelength.   As in optics, this process can be visualized as generating secondary spherical waves, and the square of the resultant wave amplitude gives a measure of the probability of the particle being scattered in a particular direction.

We can also think of an incident beam of electrons which all have the same energy as having an associated de Broglie wavelength. The diffraction of this beam of electrons by a crystal can be understood as the result of interference between the phases of the partial waves originating at the scattering centers. The square of the amplitude of the resulting wave gives the probability of the electrons being scattered at a particular angle and is a measure of the current of electrons scattered in that direction. In summary, the mechanical process of scattering is accompanied by a wave process, a guiding wave described by Schrödinger's equation, in which the square of the wave amplitude determines the probability that the process will have a particular course or direction.

The wave property of electrons has significantly modified the concepts in atomic theory. Bohr's theory assumed the electron to be a charged particle of very small size, circulating in a quantized orbit about the nucleus. The wave mechanics shows that the electron should be visualized as a wave packet of extended size and that the square of the amplitude of the wave function of the electron is a measure of the probability of the electron being in a particular location.

These concepts can be correlated by applying the wave property of particles to the atomic electrons. As a simple example, consider the electron in the hydrogen atom as a standing wave extending in a circle around the nucleus. For the electron wave just to fill the circumference of the circle, the circle must contain an integral number of wavelengths

$$2\pi r = n\lambda \qquad\qquad (3.32)$$

where $r$ is the radius of the circle and $n$ is an integer.

Now, applying de Broglie's relation for the wavelength

$$\lambda = \frac{h}{p} = \frac{h}{mv} \qquad (3.33)$$

and substituting in Eq. (3.32), we obtain

$$2\pi r = n\frac{h}{mv} \qquad \text{or} \qquad mvr = n\frac{h}{2\pi} \qquad (3.34)$$

This relation is exactly the Bohr postulate for the quantization of angular momentum given in Eq. (3.3), if we now associate the number of wavelengths in the standing wave with the principal quantum number in Bohr's theory. This visualization of an atomic electron is illustrated in Fig. 3.10.

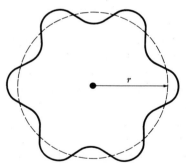

**Fig. 3.10**   *Visualization of an electron standing wave pattern in a Bohr orbit for which n = 6. Where is the electron?*

The wave function of an atomic electron can be obtained by solving the Schrödinger wave equation in three dimensions, using the potential energy and total energy, with boundary conditions which represent standing waves to describe the bound electron. The square of the amplitude of the wave function determines the probability that the electron will be at a particular location in the orbit at a specific time. So the electron can be conceived not as existing in any one location in the orbit but as a distribution of probabilities spread out around the entire orbit. The electron becomes a fuzzy cloud—a probability distribution. The amazing feature is that, despite this major change in our

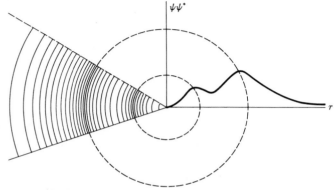

**Fig. 3.11** *Visualization of the probability amplitude $\psi\psi^*$ of two atomic electrons in quantized energy levels as a function of radius r.*

conceptual understanding of the electron, the Bohr theory, which was based on conservation of energy and momentum for a classical mass-point particle, gave such a highly precise prediction of atomic energy states.

In order to form a homogeneous theory which incorporates both wave and particle properties, it has been necessary to give up or modify some other concepts of the classical theories of both waves and particles. One of the most important of these modifications was formulated by Heisenberg in 1927 in his *uncertainty principle*. This principle states that we cannot simultaneously identify the position of a particle and its momentum with any arbitrarily desired accuracy. To measure its position with precision we must treat the particle as a mass point; to measure momentum we must know its wavelength with precision, which requires an extremely long wave train. Either precision measurement is possible (in principle), but they require separate experiments designed to measure, in one case, the particle properties, and, in the other case, the wave properties. Heisenberg showed by a rigorous derivation that the ultimate uncertainty in measurement of momentum, $\Delta p$, and simultaneously in measurement of position or length, $\Delta x$, is given by

$$\Delta x \, \Delta p \simeq h \qquad (3.35)$$

where $h$ is Planck's constant. This absolute limit of Planck's constant can be approached by increased perfection of measurement, but it can never be passed.

The motivation for the uncertainty principle can be traced to the wave property of the atomic electrons. The concept of an electron wavelength leads to an uncertainty in the azimuthal location of the electron in the orbit of a magnitude given by the wavelength of a standing wave, which is $2\pi r/n$ for $n > 1$. The uncertainty in momentum is that between one allowed orbit and the next ($n$ or $n + 1$) and has the magnitude $mv$. So the uncertainty principle can be written, in this case, as

$$\Delta p \, \Delta x \simeq mv \, \frac{2\pi r}{n} = h \qquad (3.36)$$

This relation is just another statement of the Bohr quantization relation [Eq. (3.3)]. In other words, the uncertainty principle is equivalent to the Bohr quantization relation, when the wave properties of the electron are considered.

An analogous relation can be derived for the limit of precision in the measurement of energy $\Delta E$ and of time $\Delta t$

$$\Delta E \, \Delta t \simeq h \qquad (3.37)$$

An example of this relation is the determination of the precise time of emission of a light quantum of energy $E = h\nu$ in an atomic

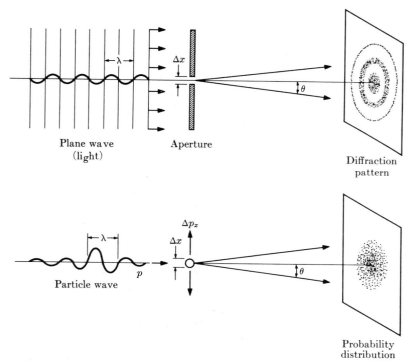

Plane wave (light)

Aperture

Diffraction pattern

Particle wave

Probability distribution

**Fig. 3.12** *Visualization of uncertainty principle: A beam of light or particles with wavelength $\lambda$ and momentum $p = h/\lambda$, limited to a transverse width $\Delta x$, has a diffraction pattern with an opening angle: $\theta \sim \lambda/\Delta x$. The uncertainty in transverse momentum is $\Delta p_x \sim p\theta = (h/\lambda)(\lambda/\Delta x) = h/\Delta x$. So, $\Delta p_x \Delta x \sim h$.*

transition. If the frequency of the light is to be measured to high precision, the wave train must be very long; but if we attempt to determine the instant in time when the event occurred, it necessarily requires some mark (hump?) on the wave train and so reduces the precision of the frequency measurement.

In atomic theory, the classical mechanics is now replaced by the wave mechanics. The duality of nature, first observed and applied to the wave and particle characteristics of light, is now extended to the particles of the atomic system. All waves have particle properties and all particles have wave properties. The two views are complementary in that it is impossible at the same time to prove the corpuscular and the wave character with arbitrary precision, but only within the limits set by the uncertainty principle. Within this domain we must forego the possibility of experimental knowledge of the intimate details of atomic processes and interactions.

### STATISTICS OF PARTICLES

Statistical mechanics is the field of physics related to the behavior of large numbers of particles. In classical mechanics the distribution of thermal velocities and energies among the molecules of a gas, in thermal equilibrium due to the exchange of energy in random impacts, is described by the Maxwell-Boltzmann statistics. If particles can exist only in a set of quantized energy states, statistical mechanics can be used to give the relative numbers of atoms or molecules in each energy state. The relative number occupying each quantized energy state, under thermal equilibrium, is given by the Boltzmann distribution formula.

Quantum mechanics has introduced two new forms of statistics, the Bose-Einstein and the Fermi-Dirac statistics. The type of quantum statistics which applies to a system of particles (all of one kind) is related to the symmetry properties of the wave function describing this system of particles. These symmetry properties have to do with the effect on the wave function of interchanging all of the coordinates of two identical particles, which is equivalent to exchanging one particle with another, say two protons in a nucleus. The coordinates which are interchanged are the three spatial coordinates and the vector direction of spin.

Fermi-Dirac statistics apply to systems of particles for which the wave function is *antisymmetric;* that is, it changes sign when all the coordinates of any pair of identical particles are interchanged. The new wave function will be identical except for a change in sign; the probability distribution of the wave function, which depends on the square of the amplitude, does not change. It can be shown that this antisymmetric property restricts the number of particles occupying each quantum state to one. That is, the Pauli principle applies for particles obeying the Fermi-Dirac statistics. It is found experimentally that electrons, protons, and neutrons are all *fermions* and that they have intrinsic spin $s = \frac{1}{2}(h/2\pi)$. Nuclei with odd mass number $A$ (total of protons and neutrons) obey the Fermi-Dirac statistics and have total angular momenta which are odd half-integral multiples of $h/2\pi$.

In the Bose-Einstein statistics the wave function is symmetrical; that is, it does not change sign when the coordinates of any pair of identical particles are exchanged. Two or more particles of this type can occupy the same quantum state. Particles which obey the Bose-Einstein statistics are called *bosons* and have zero or integral intrinsic spins. The observable particles called *mesons* (pions, kaons, etc.; see Chap. 4) are bosons and have zero spin. Nuclei which have an even number of nucleons are bosons and also have zero or integral total angular momenta. Bosons do not obey the Pauli exclusion principle.

In the chapters to follow we will find that all particles in nature are either fermions or bosons and that this property of their statistics is basic in distinguishing the several classes of particles.

# chapter 4

# OTHER ELEMENTARY PARTICLES

NATURE IS NOT CONTENT with just the components of atoms. Even so, the three fundamental particles of which atoms are formed—the proton, the neutron, and the electron—have a special significance. All stable, inert atoms are formed of these components. To the best of our knowledge, the proton and electron are absolutely stable and can never decay into lighter particles. In the free state the neutron is unstable and decays into a proton, an electron, and a neutrino (see below) with a halflife of 700 sec. However, when bound in a nucleus with protons and other neutrons, the neutron is also stable and has an infinite lifetime in all but radioactive atoms.

## THE POSITRON

During the fruitful decade of the 1930s several discoveries were made which added new and different particles to the list. P. M. Dirac in 1928 developed a relativistic, quantum-mechanical description of the electron, which considered the *negative-energy* states inherent in the wave equation by using basic theoretical symmetry considerations. He interpreted his results to indicate the possible existence of a particle with electronic charge and mass but with a positive charge $q$. One way of understanding the negative-energy states is that they represent a continuum completely filled with electrons. Since transitions cannot occur between ordinary positive-energy states and these filled negative-energy states, they are not observed in ordinary phenomena. However, if sufficient energy is available to lift an electron out of this continuum into a positive-energy state, it will leave a hole in the continuum which will have all the appearances and properties of a positively charged electron. This has the effect of producing, out of energy, a pair of electrons, one with negative and one with positive charge.    The amount of energy required is the mass energy of the two particles, which is 1.02 MeV.    Such a particle produced from the negative-energy continuum is called an *antiparticle*.

Meanwhile, C. D. Anderson of California Institute of Technology was studying cosmic rays using a cloud chamber with a superimposed magnetic field in which charged particle tracks would be curved.    In 1932 Anderson obtained a photographic picture of a track which traversed a lead plate placed across the chamber (see Fig. 4.1).    The track had different cur-

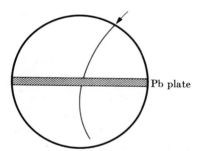

Pb plate

**Fig.  4.1**    *Illustration  of  a cloud-chamber  photograph  by  Anderson  in  1932  which  established the  existence  of  the  positron.    The track  was  curved  by  the  magnetic field  indicating  a  positive  charge but  traversed  the  lead  plate  with an  energy  loss  equal  to  that  of  an electron.*

vatures on the two sides of the plate, indicating the direction of the incoming particle.    The energy loss in the lead plate identified it as a particle of electronic mass.    However, the observed curvatures in the magnetic field could only be produced by a particle of positive charge.    Scientists quickly associated this particle with the Dirac particle, and it was given the name *positron*.

The discovery in 1934 by Curie and Joliot of nuclear disintegrations produced by $\alpha$ particles in several of the light elements that resulted in radioactive nuclei opened a new era in nuclear physics. These "artificially" produced radioactive nuclei decayed, in most instances, with the emission of positrons with characteristic half-lives of a few minutes or hours. For example, when boron is bombarded by $\alpha$ particles, the nucleus $N^{13}$ is formed, which decays into $C^{13}$ with the emission of a positron

$$_5B^{10} + {}_2He^4 \rightarrow {}_7N^{13} + {}_0n^1$$
$$_7N^{13} \rightarrow {}_6C^{13} + {}_1e^0 \qquad (T = 14 \text{ min})$$

$(4.1)$

This discovery was soon followed up by scientists using particle beams produced in accelerators, first with the cyclotron at the University of California by E. O. Lawrence and his associates and later by others. Induced radioactivities were observed from essentially all light elements by using accelerated beams of protons, deuterons, and He ions; some were "neutron-rich" isotopes which decayed with the emission of electrons, and some were "neutron-poor" which emitted positrons. Their half-lives ranged from seconds to many years.

As indicated above, the positron was immediately accepted by scientists as another fundamental particle. A further theoretical prediction was soon confirmed: that the positron would combine with an electron, after being slowed down by interactions in matter, with the release of the mass energy of the pair in the form of photons

$$e^+ + e^- \rightarrow \gamma + \gamma$$

$(4.2)$

In most cases only two photons are emitted in positron "annihilation," each with an energy of 0.51 MeV (rest energy of an electron). However, the positron did not fit in the atom with the other elementary particles. It had the much deeper significance of being an example of a completely new type of particle, which could be created and destroyed. It was the first of the class known as *antiparticles* and has been given the symbol $e^+$.

## NEUTRINOS

Another problem which challenged physicists in the 1930s was the beta decay process in natural radioactivity among the heavy elements, which seemed to violate conservation of energy and momentum. For example, in RaE the $\beta$ particles (electrons) are emitted with a spectrum of energies extending up to an end point energy of 1.17 MeV (see Fig. 4.2). The parent and product nuclei ($RaE^{210}$ and $Po^{210}$) were known to have a fixed

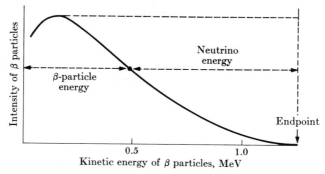

**Fig. 4.2** *β-particle spectrum of RaE and the energy assigned to neutrinos.*

mass difference regardless of the individual $\beta$-ray energies. Furthermore, by this time it was known that electrons have an intrinsic spin $s = \frac{1}{2}$ units of angular momentum. The nuclear angular momenta $I$ of the parent and product nuclei must either be the same or at the most differ by an integral unit of angular momentum, since they have the same total number of nucleons. So the emission of an electron with spin $\frac{1}{2}$ would also violate conservation of angular momentum.

Pauli proposed the hypothesis that a second, uncharged

particle was being emitted, simultaneously with the $\beta$-ray electron, which carried off the unobserved energy, momentum, and spin. In 1934 Fermi utilized this concept to develop a theory of beta decay which conserved energy and momentum and for the first time gave a quantitative explanation of the shape of the $\beta$-ray spectra. Fermi christened this particle the *neutrino $\nu$*, the "little neutral one." The properties assumed for the neutrino were zero charge, zero or very small mass, and half-integral intrinsic spin. The $\beta$-ray electron and the neutrino were assumed to be created and ejected simultaneously (see Fig. 4.3).

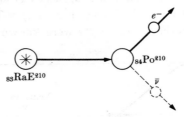

**Fig. 4.3**    *Beta decay of RaE.*

Beta decay can be considered a process in which one of the neutrons in the nucleus is transformed into a proton

$$n \rightarrow p^+ + e^- + \bar{\nu} \tag{4.3}$$

The induced radioactivities leading to positron emission, discussed in the last section, are also beta decay processes, equivalent to transforming a proton into a neutron

$$p^+ \rightarrow n + e^+ + \nu \tag{4.4}$$

(Later in this survey we will find it necessary to distinguish between the neutrinos emitted in these two processes; the one associated with the electron is called the antineutrino $\bar{\nu}$ and that with the positron is the neutrino $\nu$.)

The Fermi theory of beta decay did much more than preserve

the conservation laws. It predicted quantitatively the relative rates of decay (half-lives) of radioactive nuclei and the distribution of energy in the $\beta$-ray spectra. In Fig. 4.2 the amount of energy assigned to the neutrino in a specific process is illustrated. The conviction of physicists in the validity of the conservation laws was so basic that the existence of a zero-mass neutrino was accepted in principle for many years before it was confirmed through experimental observations. Even before it was observed, the neutrino was added to the list of elementary particles. But, like the positron, it was a particle created out of energy and not a constituent of nuclei.

Radioactive decay processes are so slow, relative to other nuclear processes, that they have been given, collectively, the name of *weak interactions*. In Chap. 2 we discussed the strong nuclear interactions and the extremely short range of nuclear forces. The time during which strong interactions occur is extremely short. An appropriate time unit is that for a particle moving with a speed close to that of light to cross a nucleon, which is about $10^{-23}$ sec. If the energy available is sufficient and momentum can be conserved, a strong interaction should take place within a small number of these nuclear time units. If the interaction involves only electromagnetic forces, the time is expected to be longer by a factor of about 100.

Fermi recognized that the very much longer lifetimes in radioactive decay processes required the existence of an interaction which was very much weaker than the nuclear or electromagnetic interactions. In terms of the nuclear time scale these radioactive decay lifetimes are enormously long. If the strong nuclear force were involved the decays would occur in nuclear times. Since this does not happen there must be some prohibition, some violation of a conservation law, which prevents the strong nuclear interaction from occurring. Yet the decays do happen eventually. So there must be another type of interaction involved which is not subject to the strong interaction conservation laws. Since the decay lifetimes are so long this new type of interaction must be much weaker. For lack of a better name it is called the weak interaction. Its relative strength is estimated to be about $10^{-13}$ of that of the strong interaction.

Neutrinos interact with other particles only through the weak interaction. They are formed in weak interaction decay processes such as those of Eqs. (4.3) and (4.4). The capture of neutrinos is also a weak interaction, with an extremely small probability. For many years it was impossible to observe the neutrino experimentally. The great difficulty in observing them was the extremely small rate of interaction with matter. Neutrinos are by far the most penetrating of all nuclear particles. In traversing the earth across a diameter only about one neutrino in $10^{10}$ will cause a reaction or be captured. The "range" of a neutrino has been estimated to be a distance equivalent to 1 light-year in lead.

Neutrinos were eventually observed only when tremendous flux densities became available from nuclear reactors, only with the use of very large volume detectors, and only at quite low counting rates. The first conclusive experiment was performed by F. Reines and R. D. Cowan in an underground room of a large reactor at Savannah River, Georgia, in 1956; they used large tanks of scintillator fluid viewed by many photomultiplier tubes to detect the scintillations caused by the charged particles resulting from the capture process. The reaction observed is the inverse of beta decay

$$\bar{\nu} + p^+ \rightarrow n + e^+ \tag{4.5}$$

This reaction was detected through the photons produced in the (delayed) capture process of the neutron and in the annihilation of the positron.

The neutrinos discussed so far are those associated with electrons and positrons. In a later section we shall discuss another type of neutrino which is associated with the decay processes of $\pi$ mesons and $\mu$ mesons; these are clearly different from electron neutrinos and are called *muon* neutrinos.

## MESONS

The origin and mechanism of the nuclear force which binds protons and neutrons in nuclei has long been the subject of theoretical speculation. H. Yukawa proposed in 1935 that it could arise from the exchange of some nuclear radiation between nucleons, analogous to the exchange of photons between electric charges which is presumed to give rise to the electromagnetic force. In nuclei the strength of the force, and its extremely short range, would require the mediating agent to be a particle of about 300 electron masses, rather than a zero-mass radiation such as the photon. The mass of such a particle, of about 150 MeV,* is intermediate between that of the electron and the proton. Particles in this mass range have been given the name *mesons*. They are sometimes described in the popular literature as the nuclear "glue" which holds nuclei together.

A charged particle with an appropriate mass was observed independently by C. D. Anderson and by J. C. Street and E. C. Stevenson in 1937 in cosmic-ray studies using cloud chambers. At first it was presumed to be the Yukawa particle responsible for the nuclear force. This assumption led to a decade of confusion before evidence accumulated to show that it was much too penetrating and its interactions with nuclei were much too weak for it to be the Yukawa particle. Not until 1947 did C. M. G. Lattes, G. Occhialini, and C. F. Powell report observing a track in photographic emulsions exposed to cosmic rays at high altitudes which had the proper grain density for a meson and which, when it was slowed down, decayed into a product meson. They called the primary particle a $\pi$ meson and the lighter product a $\mu$ meson. It is now known that the $\pi$ meson (now called the *pion*) does have the strong nuclear interaction properties of the Yukawa particle. The $\mu$ meson (now called the *muon*) is the particle first observed by Anderson and has properties similar to the electron, in all respects but its larger mass.

With the development of particle accelerators in the 200- to

* See Chap. 5 for the definition of MeV as a unit of mass.

500-MeV energy range following World War II, energies were available sufficient to create mesons in large intensities and under controllable conditions in the laboratory. The first observation of the production of pions by accelerators was by M. E. Gardner and C. M. G. Lattes in 1948, who used 380-MeV He$^{++}$ ions from the 184-in. synchrocyclotron at the University of California. Within a few years several other machines were brought into operation at energies above the threshold for production of these new particles. Pions were observed of both positive and negative charge and could be produced by protons, deuterons, He ions, neutrons, and $\gamma$ rays. The first years of operation of these accelerators were devoted largely to studies of the properties of these mesons: their mass values, energy requirements for production, production rates, and mechanisms for production and decay.

Pions are produced in nuclear interactions between a variety of bombarding particles and target nuclei. Pions of either sign of charge, $\pi^+$ and $\pi^-$, have the same mass of about 140 MeV. The bombarding energy must be larger than the rest mass for both energy and momentum to be conserved in the production process. The dynamics of momentum balance in such processes is discussed further in Chap. 5. With protons and with a dense target (high $Z$) the minimum bombarding energy (threshold energy) required to produce a single pion of low kinetic energy is about 160 MeV. If proton energy exceeds this threshold, the emitted pions have larger kinetic energies. At still higher bombarding energies a pair of pions may be produced. The single-pion production processes involve a change in sign of one of the nucleons. Some typical processes are

$$p + p \rightarrow p + n + \pi^+$$
$$p + n \rightarrow p + p + \pi^- \tag{4.6}$$
$$p + p \rightarrow p + p + \pi^+ + \pi^-$$

These are strong nuclear interactions; they have a large probability and occur in very short times.

Charged pions lose energy in absorbers in two ways, through

nuclear scattering or other nuclear interactions and through ionization of the atoms in the absorber. Energy loss through nuclear processes increases with pion energy; loss through ionization is greatest at low velocities (low energies). Eventually the pions are slowed down to thermal velocities unless they destroy themselves in flight through nuclear interactions or by decay. When slowed down, the two charged pions suffer different fates.

A slow $\pi^-$ pion can displace an electron in an atomic orbit where, because of its large mass, it occupies a very small Bohr orbit; so its wave function can overlap that of the nucleus. The $\pi^-$ pion is promptly captured by the nucleus and usually causes a nuclear disintegration in which its rest energy is distributed between several nuclear fragments. These charged nuclear fragments form a "star" in nuclear emulsions or cloud-chamber photographs, as illustrated in Fig. 4.4. The "signature" of a $\pi^-$ pion is a single track ending in a nuclear star.

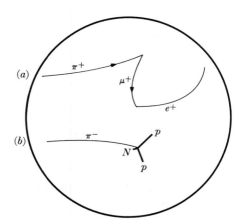

**Fig. 4.4** *Typical signatures of $\pi^+$ and $\pi^-$ pions in a cloud chamber with a magnetic field.*
*(a) $\pi^+ \rightarrow \mu^+ + \nu_\mu$; $\mu^+ \rightarrow e^+ + \nu_\mu + \nu_e$.*
*(b) $\pi^- + {}_zN^A \rightarrow {}_{z-3}N^{A-4} + p + p + n + n$.*

Positive pions $\pi^+$ are repelled by the positively charged nuclei in atoms and do not interact with atomic electrons. In matter, when $\pi^+$ pions are slowed down by ionizing impacts, they decay into positive muons and muon neutrinos

$$\pi^+ \rightarrow \mu^+ + \nu_\mu \qquad (T = 1.78 \times 10^{-8} \text{ sec}) \qquad (4.7)$$

The muon produced in the decay process is the same as the *heavy electron* or *$\mu$ meson* first observed by Anderson in cosmic rays. The range of these muons is always the same (from slow pions), indicating a two-body decay process; the energy released (34 MeV) comes from the difference in rest masses. The neutrino, however, is not the same as the one associated with electrons in beta decay processes and is given the symbol $\nu_\mu$. Evidence for this conclusion is discussed on page 76.

In the absence of matter, that is, if the pions traverse an evacuated pipe, negative pions can also decay in flight into a muon and a neutrino

$$\pi^- \rightarrow \mu^- + \overline{\nu_\mu} \qquad (T = 1.78 \times 10^{-8} \text{ sec}) \qquad (4.8)$$

Here the neutrino is the anti-muon-neutrino, indicated by the bar over the symbol. It should also be noted that the half-life of the decay process $T$ given above is valid for pions with sub-relativistic velocities; if the pions have relativistic speeds their decay lifetime is "dilated" to longer times, following the Lorentz transformation equation given in Eq. (3.13).

To complete the pion story, we should add the prediction and discovery of the neutral pion $\pi^0$. As an extension of Yukawa's theoretical speculation on the origin of nuclear forces, J. R. Oppenheimer in 1947 suggested that neutral mesons might also be involved in the exchange process between nucleons and that if such a neutral meson were ejected from a nuclear interaction it should decay very rapidly into photons. He suggested that such photons might be partially responsible for the soft showers of photons and electrons observed to be produced by cosmic rays in the atmosphere. The search for a $\pi^0$ pion was carried on in several laboratories. The most convincing evidence of their existence came from experiments with the synchrocyclotron at the University of California in 1950. Nuclear emulsions (photographic film sensitive to lightly ionizing particles such as electrons) were placed behind targets in which pions were produced by the accelerated beam. Under microscopic examination, associated pairs of electron tracks were observed close to the front surface of the emulsion. These were presumed to be produced by the photons resulting from pion decay

$$\pi^0 \rightarrow \gamma + \gamma$$

followed by $(4.9)$

$$\gamma \rightarrow e^+ + e^-$$

The tracks of the two associated electron pairs could be projected back to locate the position of the $\pi^0$ decay process. The short distance traversed by the $\pi^0$ indicated a very short half-life of about $10^{-16}$ sec (see Fig. 4.5). It might be noted that this is the shortest decay lifetime which has been measured experimentally.

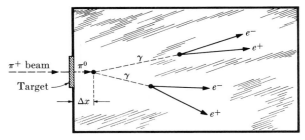

**Fig. 4.5**    *Decay of $\pi^0$ pion into two photons, observed in a photographic emulsion (greatly magnified).*

## MUONS

Now let us consider the quite different properties of the $\mu$ mesons or muons. Muons, electrons, and neutrinos form a category of particles called *leptons*, which are fermions with half-integral intrinsic spin and which interact with other particles primarily through the weak interaction. The charged leptons may also be involved in electromagnetic interactions with other charged particles and with photons. But leptons never interact with other particles through the strong nuclear interaction. For example, muons do not interact with nuclei, as pions do, but lose energy only by ionization in matter. The rate of energy loss through ionization is about 2 MeV for each g/cm² of absorbing material. The range of a muon in matter is nearly proportional to its energy. If a mixed beam of pions and muons traverses an absorber, most of the pions will be removed through nuclear interactions while the muons (if of sufficient energy) will penetrate the absorber. Muons are the "penetrating" component of the ionizing particles in cosmic radiation observed beneath great layers of earth in salt mines.

The muons produced in pion decays will be slowed down by ionizing impacts. Slow $\mu^-$ muons can also displace electrons in atomic orbits and form temporarily stable atoms. The atom parallel to hydrogen, which has a proton nucleus and a $\mu^-$ muon in an atomic orbit, has been produced and studied in the laboratory; it is called a *$\mu$-mesic* atom. Eventually, the muon decays into an electron and two neutrinos

$$\mu^- \rightarrow e^- + \bar{\nu}_e + \nu_\mu \qquad (T = 1.52 \times 10^{-6} \text{ sec}) \qquad (4.10)$$

Evidence that this is a three-body decay is that the electrons have a wide distribution in energy. Three products are also required if spin is to be conserved (see Chap. 5). The energy released (105 MeV) comes from the difference in rest masses of the muon and the electron. Note that one neutrino is of the electron family and the other is of the muon family. This is a requirement of the particle number conservation law (see Chap. 5) and is another example of the difference between electron and muon neutrinos.

The positive muon $\mu^+$ can capture an electron in a Bohr orbit and form a temporarily stable *muonium* atom. Because of the relatively long half-life of the muon the atom survives long enough to be studied in the laboratory in considerable detail.

The positive muon decays eventually into products similar to those for the negative muon

$$\mu^+ \rightarrow e^+ + \nu_e + \overline{\nu_\mu} \qquad (T = 1.52 \times 10^{-6} \text{ sec}) \qquad (4.11)$$

So the signature of a $\pi^+$ pion in an emulsion or in a cloud-chamber photograph is a sequence of three ionizing connected tracks, $\pi^+$, $\mu^+$, $e^+$, with sharp angular deflections between them; the neutrinos which are also emitted in these decays are not observed. This typical signature is illustrated in Fig. 4.4.

We indicated earlier that the neutrinos accompanying muons in pion decay differ from those associated with electrons in beta decay. At first it was assumed that these neutrinos were the same. They have the same basic properties of zero rest mass, zero charge, and half-integral spin. They both interact only through the weak interaction. This last property has made them very hard to detect. Electron neutrinos were first observed by F. Reines and C. L. Cowan through the inverse beta decay process [Eq. (4.5)] in which the neutrino is absorbed by a proton and changes it into a neutron plus a positron

$$\overline{\nu_e} + p \rightarrow n + \overline{e^+} \qquad (4.12)$$

These electron neutrinos were produced from a high-flux nuclear reactor by beta decay following neutron capture and so were electron-associated neutrinos.

Adequate fluxes of muon neutrinos have become available

only in recent years from very-high-energy proton accelerators, primarily through the decay of pions produced in targets. The experiment in which muon neutrinos were first observed was performed at Brookhaven National Laboratory in 1964 with the 32-GeV accelerator. The high-energy neutrinos were projected forward by pion decays in flight, were passed through great thicknesses of shielding to remove all muons and other charged particles, and traversed a very large *spark chamber* detector. The events observed were essentially all of the type which produced muons, which can readily be identified in the photographs.

$$\nu_\mu + n \rightarrow p + \mu^-$$

$$\overline{\nu_\mu} + p \rightarrow n + \mu^+$$

(4.13)

If these were the same as electron neutrinos, they should also have produced electrons, as in Eq. (4.12). However, the few electron events observed could all be explained by a small contamination of $\nu_e$ neutrinos. It appears that muon neutrinos cannot produce electron events and therefore differ from electron neutrinos.

The existence of two different types of neutrinos is one of the most challenging problems of particle physics at the present time. This may be the same problem as that of the weak interaction itself. If so, it may also be associated with the other basic problem of weak interactions—the question why the muon exists. At present there is no satisfactory answer to any of these problems. One tentative correlation seems to exist: in each event in which a neutrino is involved it seems to be associated with three other fermions. This can be noted in Eqs. (4.3) to (4.5), where two of the fermions are nucleons, and in Eqs. (4.10) to (4.13), where all four particles are leptons. In pion decay, Eqs. (4.7) and (4.8), it is possible to conceive, theoretically, of an intermediate state involving two virtual nucleons which produce the lepton products through the weak interaction. The significance of these correlations is still not clear.

This section has carried our discussion of mesons, muons, and neutrinos almost up to the present time. Only a fraction of this information was available in 1947, although the existence of these classes of particles had been demonstrated.

## STRANGE PARTICLES

A list of elementary particles compiled in 1947 would have included those described above with perhaps a few comments of a speculative nature by cosmic-ray experimenters on the possible existence of heavier mesons. This list with the presently known properties of these particles is shown in Table 1. The number of particles for which reasonable experimental evidence existed was 10; 4 others had been predicted on good theoretical grounds but had not yet been observed. By this time the definition of elementary particles had expanded to include more than the components of atoms. It now included particles created in nuclear decay processes, such as pions and muons, and zero-mass neutrinos; it also included antiparticles, although the positron was the only example which had been observed.

Then in a relatively few years the field of particle physics exploded! The list of elementary particles jumped to over 30 within the next 8 years. This period of great productivity was due primarily to the experimental use of a new generation of particle accelerators of much higher energy, based on the principle of phase-stable acceleration announced by V. Veksler in Moscow and (independently) by E. M. McMillan at the University of California in 1945. It was also associated with the return of physicists to their laboratories at the end of World War II and their rapid development of new techniques and new instruments for measurement, such as scintillation counters, high-speed electronic systems, and, somewhat later, the liquid-hydrogen bubble chambers.

**TABLE 1   Elementary Particles Known in 1947**

| CLASS | SYMBOL | MASS, MeV | CHARGE | SPIN | HALF-LIFE | DECAY PRODUCTS |
|---|---|---|---|---|---|---|
| Photon | $\gamma$ | 0 | 0 | 1 | Stable | |
| Neutrino | $\nu$, $\overline{(\nu)}$ | 0 | 0 | $\frac{1}{2}$ | Stable | |
| Electron | $e^-$, $e^+$ | 0.51 | $\pm q$ | $\frac{1}{2}$ | Stable | |
| $\mu$ meson | $\mu^-$, $\mu^+$ | 105.6 | $\pm q$ | $\frac{1}{2}$ | $1.5 \times 10^{-6}$ sec | $\rightarrow e^{\pm} + \nu + \nu$ |
| $\pi$ meson | $\pi^+$, $\pi^-$ | 140 | $\pm q$ | 0 | $1.8 \times 10^{-8}$ sec | $\rightarrow \mu^{\pm} + \nu$ |
| | $(\pi^0)$ | 135 | 0 | 0 | $\sim 10^{-16}$ sec | $\rightarrow \gamma + \gamma$ |
| Nucleon | $p^+$, $\overline{(p^-)}$ | 938.2 | $\pm q$ | $\frac{1}{2}$ | Stable | |
| | $n$, $\overline{(n)}$ | 939.5 | 0 | $\frac{1}{2}$ | 700 sec | $\rightarrow p^+ + e^- + \nu$ |

NOTE: ( ) = predicted, ‾ = antiparticles.

The first group of high-energy accelerators to be started after 1945 were of two types, electron synchrotrons in the energy range of 300 to 350 MeV and synchrocyclotrons which could accelerate protons, deuterons, or $He^{++}$ ions to energies of 150 to 450 MeV. Within a few years six electron synchrotrons and six synchrocyclotrons were under construction in the United States, with others in Europe and in the U.S.S.R. By 1948 the first of these high-energy machines were completed and starting to produce scientific results. Among the first of these results was the production of pions with the 184-in. synchrocyclotron at the University of California. Soon it was possible to produce beams of pions of known and controllable energy, in sufficient intensity to use them as secondary beams for observing their nuclear interactions and other properties.

Meanwhile, designs and construction were started for two proton synchrotrons in the United States which could produce protons of multibillion-volt (multi-GeV*) energy. By 1955 the Brookhaven cosmotron had been in operation for several years at 3-GeV energy, and the bevatron at the University of California had been completed at 6 GeV. With these multibillion-volt accelerators it was possible to produce and study particles with mass values greater than nucleons. Several new families of particles were discovered with properties of a completely unpredicted and "strange" nature. A number of extremely short-lived particle states called *resonances* were disclosed and their properties studied (see Chap. 10).

Then the floodgates closed as suddenly as they had opened. In the years since 1955, only two new particles and a few missing members of existing families have been added. Progress has come largely through extension of our understanding of resonances.

The first evidence for the many new particles, first called *strange*, came from tracks observed in photographs of cloud

* *The symbol GeV (giga electron volt) is used internationally to represent an energy unit of 1000 MeV. The symbol BeV (billion electron volt) is also used in the United States.*

chambers exposed to cosmic rays at a high-altitude laboratory, reported by G. D. Rochester and C. C. Butler of the University of Manchester in 1947. This evidence was the observation of V tracks consisting of two charged-particle tracks coming from a common origin, of which one was identified as a proton and the other as a negative pion. The neutral particle which decayed to give these products, now called the *lambda-zero*, ($\Lambda^0$), must have had a mass greater than the sum of proton and pion masses. Such a neutral particle would not cause ionization in the chamber and so would not be observed (see Fig. 4.6). This was the first

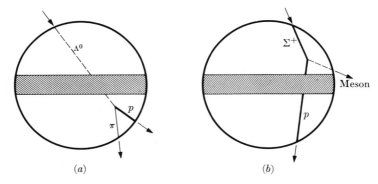

(a)                                        (b)

**Fig. 4.6**    *Evidence of strange particles produced by cosmic rays.*
*(a) A neutral particle decays in flight into two charged particles (V track).    (b) A charged heavy particle decays into a neutral particle and another heavy charged particle.*

convincing evidence for a particle heavier than a nucleon. Another observation was a single track which showed a sharp change in direction and a reduction in grain density in which the secondary track was also identified as a proton. This track was interpreted as a charged heavy particle (now called the $\Sigma^+$) decaying into a proton and a neutral meson which was not observed. But the real explosion of experimental evidence for these many new particles started about 1953 with accelerator studies using the 3-GeV cosmotron at Brookhaven.

The Brookhaven experiments used high-energy charged pions coming from a target in the cosmotron which were directed into a liquid-hydrogen bubble chamber with a superimposed magnetic field. The nuclear interactions of the pions with protons in the hydrogen had a large yield and many kinds of particles were produced. Photographs of the charged-particle tracks were analyzed to determine their momenta and to identify the particles.

The new particles were of two basic types: *k* mesons with mass values less than nucleon mass, now called *kaons*; and *hyperons*, with masses greater than the nucleon mass. They were observed to be produced in pairs in a "fast" nuclear interaction and then to separate and decay at a much slower rate associated with the weak interaction. Occasionally, one of these new particles in flight would have a strong interaction with a nucleon, producing still other kinds of particles. An early and typical example of the associated production of two strange particles observed at Brookhaven in 1954 was the production of two previously unknown neutral particles, the *K*-zero and the lambda-zero, each of which decayed into a pair of known charged particles. This example is described further in Chap. 9 and illustrated in Fig. 9.1.

These particles were called strange because of their unusual behavior. They were produced in high-energy collisions of strongly interacting particles such as pions and nucleons, with a high probability (large cross section) compatible with the strong nuclear interaction; the time associated with such a strong interaction is that required for a particle having the velocity of light to traverse a nucleon, which is of the order of $10^{-23}$ sec. Yet the product strange particles had very much longer lifetimes, decaying into lighter-mass products with lifetimes of $10^{-8}$ to $10^{-11}$ sec. This indicated that the decay process was not a fast nuclear interaction but a much weaker interaction. The analysis of this evidence, which led to the new conservation principle called *strangeness*, is discussed more fully in Chap. 9.

During these years four classes of strange particles were

identified and fitted into their strangeness categories. The kaon class $K$ were mesons with mass values of about half that of nucleons and consisted of positive, neutral, and negative members. Three classes were found which were heavier than nucleons (called hyperons), with ascending mass values. The first is the neutral lambda-zero ($\Lambda^0$), called a *singlet* since it occurs only in the neutral form. Another is the set of three sigma particles ($\Sigma$) (a *triplet*) with positively charged, neutral, and negatively charged members of closely similar mass values. The third is the xi-particle ($\Xi$), a *doublet* with neutral and negatively charged members.

The existence of the eta-zero ($\eta^0$) meson, which decays into three pions with a very short lifetime, was proposed in 1960 to explain the observed energy distributions of pions coming from very-high-energy interactions. And one further class of hyperons, the omega-minus ($\Omega^-$) singlet, was discovered in 1964 with a mass higher than all the others. With these, there are now six classes of particles to be added to those listed in Table 1. Their mass values, quantum numbers, and other distingushing properties are now well known. The original term *strange particles* to describe these new classes of particles has become obsolete. The term survives only in the use of the principle of conservation of strangeness in the strong interactions, which is discussed in Chap. 9.

### ANTIPARTICLES

Another experimental breakthrough came with the observation of antiprotons and antineutrons with the 6-GeV bevatron at the University of California in 1957. The existence of these antinucleons was anticipated as an extension of the Dirac theory which had predicted the existence of the positron. The bevatron had been designed to reach the necessary energy thresholds for production of antiprotons and antineutrons. Evidence that antiprotons ($\overline{p^-}$) had been produced came through observation of multiprong stars formed in a liquid-hydrogen bubble chamber when the antiparticles were slowed down sufficiently for them to combine with a nórmal proton.  The total energy in the observed ionizing fragments from the stars (plus the nonionizing neutral particles which were assumed also to be produced) was far greater than the energy of the incoming particle and could be explained only by the energy of annihilation; a typical process is

$$\overline{p^-} + p \rightarrow x(\pi^+) + x(\pi^-) + y(\pi^0) \qquad (4.14)$$

where the mass energy of the two protons (plus the incoming kinetic energy) is shared between the mass energies and kinetic energies of $x$ pairs of charged pions and $y$ neutral pions.  This example is illustrated in Fig. 10.2 and the process is discussed in more detail in Chap. 10.

This evidence justifies the generalization that for each particle there will be an antiparticle, differing in some fundamental way.  When the particle is charged, the antiparticle has opposite charge; for example, the $\mu^+$ is the antiparticle of the $\mu^-$, and the $\pi^-$ is the antiparticle of the $\pi^+$.  Neutral particles also have antiparticles, characterized by reversed signs of the quantum numbers for particle number (see Chap. 5), isotopic spin (Chap. 8), and strangeness (Chap. 9).  Antiparticles are presumed to have the same mass values as their particles and the same lifetimes (in the absence of other interactions).  When conditions allow, an antiparticle will combine with its normal particle twin with the release of their total mass energy in other forms of energy.  Annihilations have been observed for positrons, negative protons, and antineutrons.  Antiparticles have been observed experimentally or are assumed for most of the known particles.  However, there are exceptions to this general rule that each particle has an antiparticle.  These exceptions are the uncharged bosons, the $\gamma$, $\pi^0$, and $\eta^0$; for these three particles there is no distinction between particle and antiparticle—they are their own antiparticles.

The accepted symbol to describe antiparticles is a bar over the symbol for the particle (i.e., $\overline{K^0}$). The symbol is needed and is consistently used for neutral antiparticles. However, for many others the sign of the charge is sufficient identification (i.e., $e^+$, $p^-$, $\mu^+$, $\pi^-$) and the bar symbol is not necessary. In the discussions and analyses which follow it is used only when the distinction is essential to the argument.

### CLASSIFICATIONS

At the present time (1967), the number of particles which can be distinguished through their different mass values, different charges, or some other basic quantum number is so great that the term *elementary* is hardly justified. The present belief of most physicists is that few, if any, of these particles deserve the title "elementary." The simple concept of a few elementary particles of which all composite systems are formed is giving way to a more general concept in which all particles are considered similar in being possible states in which energy can "condense," that they differ in the properties defined by a limited number of quantum numbers and selection rules, and that they are all components of a few simple systems based on broad symmetry principles. This concept is discussed further in Chap. 12.

However, there is still a desire to classify and tabulate those particles which are the closest to being elementary, those which have lifetimes sufficiently long so they can be observed experimentally as entities in counters, bubble chambers, or photographic emulsions. Most of these particles have lifetimes in the range $10^{-6}$ to $10^{-11}$ sec. This time is sufficient to allow the shortest lived to travel a few centimeters or a few millimeters. A few, such as the $\pi^0$, have still shorter lifetimes of about $10^{-16}$ sec, which can be measured by use of special experimental techniques. This characteristic of existence as entities long enough for their properties to be observed and measured allows a somewhat arbitrary selection of the "observable" particles, which are presented in Table 2 on pages 86 and 87.

The observable particles can be separated into four major classes which form a rising scale of mass values. These classes are *photon, lepton, meson,* and *baryon.* Two of the groups are *fermions* (leptons and baryons) with half-integral intrinsic spin that obey the Fermi-Dirac statistics and the Pauli exclusion principle. The other two groups are *bosons* (the photon and mesons) with zero or integral spin that obey the Bose-Einstein statistics. Fermions are subject to a conservation principle by which they can be created or destroyed only in conjunction with an antiparticle of the same class. For example, when an electron is emitted from a nucleus in a beta decay process, it is accompanied by an antineutrino. This conservation principle does not apply to bosons; as long as charge, angular momentum, etc., are conserved, bosons can be created in any number allowed by the available energy. For example, $K$ mesons can decay into either two or three lighter mesons. But if a boson decays into leptons it must be into two leptons, one a particle and one an antiparticle.

Table 2 lists those particles with lifetimes greater than $10^{-16}$ sec and their more important properties. These properties include mass (in MeV units), intrinsic spin, parity, isotopic spin and its third component, baryon number, lepton number, strangeness, half-life, and the principal modes of decay. The electric charge is indicated by a superscript ($^+$, $^-$, $^0$) on the particle symbol; for convenience the charge symbol is usually omitted for the proton ($p$) and electron ($e$). The four classes of particles described above are separated by solid lines in Table 2. Symbols for the antiparticles are indicated in the right-hand side in the column of symbols, and the values of those properties which differ between particles and antiparticles are tabulated on the right-hand side of the appropriate columns. One purpose of this survey is to describe these and other known properties of the particles listed in Table 2 and to discuss the correlations and some of the more definitive experimental evidence for these properties.

**TABLE 2  The Observable Particles**

| CLASS | SYMBOL | MASS, MeV $M$ | SPIN $s$ | PARITY $P$ | ISOTOPIC SPIN $I$ | $I_3$ | PARTICLE NUMBER BARYON $A$ | LEPTON $L$ | STRANGENESS $S$ | HALF-LIFE, sec $T$ | PRINCIPAL DECAY MODES |
|---|---|---|---|---|---|---|---|---|---|---|---|
| *Photon* | $\gamma$ | 0 | 1 | $-1$ | — | — | 0 | 0 | 0 | — | Stable |
| *Lepton* | $\nu_e, \overline{\nu}_e$ | 0 | $\frac{1}{2}$ | — | — | — | 0 | $1, -1$ | — | — | Stable |
| | $\nu_\mu, \overline{\nu}_\mu$ | 0 | $\frac{1}{2}$ | — | — | — | 0 | $1, -1$ | — | — | Stable |
| | $e^-, \overline{e^+}$ | 0.51098 | $\frac{1}{2}$ | 1 | — | — | 0 | $1, -1$ | — | — | Stable |
| | $\mu^-, \overline{\mu^+}$ | 105.653 | $\frac{1}{2}$ | 1 | — | — | 0 | $1, -1$ | — | $1.52 \times 10^{-6}$ | $\mu^\pm \rightarrow e^\pm + \nu_e + \nu_\mu$ |
| *Meson* | $\pi^+, \pi^-$ | 139.58 | 0 | $-1$ | 1 | $1, -1$ | 0 | 0 | 0 | $1.78 \times 10^{-8}$ | $\pi^\pm \rightarrow \mu^\pm + \nu_\mu$ |
| | $\pi^0$ | 134.99 | 0 | $-1$ | 1 | 0 | 0 | 0 | 0 | $0.7 \times 10^{-16}$ | $\pi^0 \rightarrow \gamma + \gamma$ |
| | $K^+, \overline{K^-}$ | 493.8 | 0 | $-1$ | $\frac{1}{2}$ | $\frac{1}{2}, -\frac{1}{2}$ | 0 | 0 | $1, -1$ | $0.8 \times 10^{-8}$ | $K^\pm \rightarrow \pi^\pm + \pi^0$ ; $K^\pm \rightarrow \pi^\pm + \pi^+ + \pi^-$ |
| | $K^0, \overline{K^0}$ | 497.8 | 0 | $-1$ | $\frac{1}{2}$ | $\frac{1}{2}, -\frac{1}{2}$ | 0 | 0 | $1, -1$ | $0.7 \times 10^{-10}$ ; $4 \times 10^{-8}$ | $K_1^0 \rightarrow \pi^+ + \pi^-$ ; $K_2^0 \rightarrow \pi^+ + \pi^- + \pi^0$ |
| | $\eta^0$ | 548 | 0 | $-1$ | 0 | 0 | 0 | 0 | 0 | $(<10^{-16})_{J_1}$ | $\eta^0 \rightarrow \pi^+ + \pi^- + \pi^0$ |

**TABLE 2  The Observable Particles (Continued)**

| CLASS | SYMBOL | MASS, MeV $M$ | SPIN $s$ | PARITY $P$ | ISOTOPIC SPIN $I$ | $I_3$ | PARTICLE NUMBER BARYON $A$ | LEPTON $L$ | STRANGENESS $S$ | HALF-LIFE, sec $T$ | PRINCIPAL DECAY MODES |
|---|---|---|---|---|---|---|---|---|---|---|---|
| *Nucleon* | $p^+, \bar{p}^-$ | 938.21 | $\frac{1}{2}$ | 1 | $\frac{1}{2}$ | $\frac{1}{2}, -\frac{1}{2}$ | $1, -1$ | 0 | $0, 0$ | — | Stable |
| | $n, \bar{n}$ | 939.50 | $\frac{1}{2}$ | 1 | $\frac{1}{2}$ | $-\frac{1}{2}, +\frac{1}{2}$ | $1, -1$ | 0 | $0, 0$ | $0.71 \times 10^3$ | $n \to p^+ + e^- + \nu_e$ |
| *Baryon* | $\Lambda^0, \bar{\Lambda}^0$ | 1115.4 | $\frac{1}{2}$ | 1 | 0 | 0 | $1, -1$ | 0 | $-1, +1$ | $1.8 \times 10^{-10}$ | $\Lambda^0 \to p^+ + \pi^-$ $\Lambda^0 \to n + \pi^0$ |
| | $\Sigma^+, \bar{\Sigma}^-$ | 1189.2 | $\frac{1}{2}$ | 1 | 1 | $1, -1$ | $1, -1$ | 0 | $-1, +1$ | $0.6 \times 10^{-10}$ | $\Sigma^+ \to p^+ + \pi^0$ $\Sigma^+ \to n + \pi^+$ |
| | $\Sigma^-, \bar{\Sigma}^+$ | 1197.6 | $\frac{1}{2}$ | 1 | 1 | $-1, +1$ | $1, -1$ | 0 | $-1, +1$ | $1.2 \times 10^{-10}$ | $\Sigma^- \to n + \pi^-$ |
| | $\Sigma^0, \bar{\Sigma}^0$ | 1193.2 | $\frac{1}{2}$ | 1 | 1 | $0, 0$ | $1, -1$ | 0 | $-1, +1$ | $<10^{-14}$ | $\Sigma^0 \to \Lambda^0 + \gamma$ |
| | $\Xi^-, \bar{\Xi}^+$ | 1321.0 | $\frac{1}{2}$ | 1 | $\frac{1}{2}$ | $-\frac{1}{2}, +\frac{1}{2}$ | $1, -1$ | 0 | $-2, +2$ | $0.9 \times 10^{-10}$ | $\Xi^- \to \Lambda^0 + \pi^-$ |
| | $\Xi^0, \bar{\Xi}^0$ | 1310 | $\frac{1}{2}$ | 1 | $\frac{1}{2}$ | $-\frac{1}{2}, -\frac{1}{2}$ | $1, -1$ | 0 | $-2, +2$ | $1.0 \times 10^{-10}$ | $\Xi^0 \to \Lambda^0 + \pi^0$ |
| | $\Omega^-, \bar{\Omega}^+$ | 1675 | $\frac{3}{2}$ | 1 | 0 | $0, 0$ | $1, -1$ | 0 | $-3, +3$ | $\sim 10^{-10}$ | $\Omega^- \to \Xi^0 + \pi^0 + K^0$ |

The number of *observable* particles listed in Table 2 is 35; this includes 16 pairs of particles and antiparticles and the $\gamma$, $\pi^0$, and $\eta^0$ which are their own antiparticles and are counted only once. There are reasons to believe that this list of particles with lifetimes long enough to be observed as entities is approaching completeness. Nevertheless, the number is clearly so large that the term "elementary" is hardly justified. But this tabulation does have a type of uniqueness. Each of the strongly inter-acting particles listed (mesons and baryons, which are collectively called *hadrons*) has the lowest allowed value of intrinsic spin for the class (i.e., 0 for bosons and $\frac{1}{2}$ for fermions), with one exception, the $\Omega^-$ which has a spin of $\frac{3}{2}$. Higher spin states (i.e., 1, 2, . . . for bosons and $\frac{3}{2}$, $\frac{5}{2}$, . . . for fermions) occur for the resonance states discussed in Chap. 10, which are not listed here.

*chapter 5*

# CONSERVATION
# LAWS

CONSERVATION LAWS ARE BASIC LAWS OF NATURE which have been formulated by scientists to "explain" why some processes occur in nature and others do not occur. They are essential first steps in the search for order and fundamental principles. The first four of these conservation laws were recognized during the era of classical science to explain the large-scale phenomena observable with the crude instruments of a hundred years ago. These classical conservation principles describe the conservation of energy, of linear momentum, of angular momentum, and of electric charge. In order to formulate these laws scientists conceived and defined such qualities of matter as energy, momentum, and charge. Methods of measurement of these qualities had to be devised and acceptable units established. Occasionally, with new experimental evidence, it has been necessary to revise or extend the definitions to retain the generality or "legality" of the conservation laws.

These laws are formulated by men, and the qualities of matter required to express them are concepts of the human mind. Nevertheless, they serve the essential purpose of providing simple descriptions of the complicated events we observe. The test of their validity comes in the consistency and generality with which they predict and explain observations. The four conservation laws dating from the classical era of science have served us well. With our present definitions and understandings, there are no examples in nature in which these four conservation laws are violated. They are as valid in the interactions of single, high-energy particles as they are in the macroscopic world.

## CONSERVATION OF ENERGY

In classical physics, the concept of energy conservation became possible when heat was recognized as a form of energy. When the temperature of an object was identified with the random thermal motions of its molecular components, it became possible to define thermal energy and to measure the mechanical equivalent of heat. Other forms of mechanical energy, such as the kinetic energy of motion ($\frac{1}{2}mv^2$) and the potential energy due to position in the earth's gravitational field ($mgh$), had previously been recognized and correlated. The first statement of the law of conservation of energy was that in any closed mechanical system the sum of the kinetic, gravitational, and thermal energies remains constant.

When the energy involved in chemical reactions was recognized and became measurable, the potential energy of molecular bonds was added to the list. With a growing understanding of electromagnetic phenomena, the energy stored in electric and magnetic fields was included. The development of atomic theory added the quantized energy states of electrons in atoms. The light quantum, or photon, emitted in atomic transitions was found in each case to have a discrete energy, $E = h\nu$, where $h$ is Planck's constant and $\nu$ is the frequency. Energy was observed to be conserved in the excitation of atoms and in the radiation of light from atoms. Then, with the theory of relativity and early studies of atomic disintegrations, it became necessary to include the energy associated with mass through the Einstein equivalence relation, $E = mc^2$. In its present form the law of conservation of energy includes the energy equivalent of mass of all components involved in an interaction.

In applying the conservation law to nuclear disintegrations or high-energy particle interactions, the gravitational, thermal, and chemical energies are so small that they can be omitted from the energy balance. In nuclear physics the most common form of the conservation law is the *Q-equation*. In a nuclear disintegration such as $a + b \rightarrow c + d$, in which the incoming kinetic energy is $T_a$ and the products have kinetic energies $T_c$ and $T_d$ (the target $b$ being at rest), the energy change comes from the change in rest mass

$$Q = T_c + T_d - T_a = [(m_a + m_b) - (m_c + m_d)]c^2 \qquad (5.1)$$

Energy change $Q$ is positive (exoergic) if mass decreases. $Q$ can be negative if mass increases. In nuclear physics the units commonly used for kinetic energy are million electron volts (MeV). Masses are expressed in atomic mass units (amu), which are the masses of the neutral atoms involved. The amu is $\frac{1}{16}$ the mass of a neutral $O^{16}$ atom, on the physical* mass scale in which 1 mole of $O^{16} = 16.0000$ g. The conversion factor is 1 amu $= 931.16$ MeV (see Chap. 6). This mass scale is convenient since most atomic mass values are given approximately by the atomic number; that is, $m_{H^1} = 1.008142$ amu, $m_{He^4} = 4.003873$, $m_{C^{12}} = 12.003804$, etc.

In particle physics the method of utilizing the energy conservation principle is even more direct. The $Q$-equation is the basic formulation and relates energy change to change in mass. However, since in particle physics we deal with single particles, the particle masses are also expressed directly in MeV units. With both energy and mass expressed in MeV units the number of symbols and the complexity of the equations can be reduced. For example, the relativistic expression for total energy $E$ of a particle of rest mass $m_0$ and kinetic energy $T$ is

$$E = mc^2 = \frac{m_0 c^2}{(1 - v^2/c^2)^{\frac{1}{2}}} = m_0 c^2 + T \qquad (5.2a)$$

By using MeV units for both energy and mass, we have

$$E = m = \frac{m_0}{(1 - \beta^2)^{\frac{1}{2}}} = m_0 + T \qquad (5.2b)$$

Here we have adopted a convention in which the velocity of light $c = 1$ and the velocity of the particle is expressed as a dimensionless quantity $\beta = v/c$ which is always smaller than unity. It will be convenient to make occasional use of this

---

* *Note that this differs from the "chemical" mass scale in which 1 mole of $C^{12} = 12.0000$ g.*

system of units in which the unit of mass is 1 MeV, $c = 1$, and $\beta < 1$, in order to make formulations more concise.

In a typical high-energy particle interaction, $a + b \rightarrow c + d$, where the mass of one of the product particles (say $c$) is unknown, the $Q$-equation gives

$$m_c = (m_a + m_b) - m_d + T_a - (T_c + T_d) \tag{5.3}$$

Excited particle states or resonances are characterized by larger mass values than for the known (observable) particles. The magnitude of the excitation of such a heavier particle is given by the "missing mass" calculated from the $Q$-equation when the mass of the normal particle is assumed.

In an interaction in which the product particles have greater mass than the incident particles, there will be a threshold energy $(T_a)_{\min}$ below which the process cannot proceed

$$(T_a)_{\min} \geq (m_c + m_d) - (m_a + m_b)^* \tag{5.4}$$

At this threshold the kinetic energies of the product particles will be zero. For example, in electron-pair production by photons, which can occur only in the presence of a nuclear field $N$ (because of other conservation laws), the photon energy must equal or exceed the mass energy of the pair, which is 1.02 MeV. The process can be written

$$\gamma + N \rightarrow N + e^- + e^+ \tag{5.5}$$

In the decay of a particle at rest, after it has been slowed down by collisions with other particles or by ionization, into two or more product particles, $a \rightarrow c + d + \cdots$, we have

$$m_a = m_c + m_d + \cdots + T_c + T_d + \cdots \tag{5.6}$$

*See the following section for the reason for the inequality.

The sum of the masses of the product particles must be less than the mass of the parent particle for the decay to occur; otherwise the decay into this set of products is forbidden.

It might be argued that the validity of the law of conservation of mass energy is a consequence of our definitions and that all we have accomplished is to define certain qualities of nature which obey this law. This in itself is a major intellectual triumph in that such a simple hypothesis can explain and correlate so many diverse phenomena. We are certainly justified in assuming that this law represents a basic attribute of nature.

### CONSERVATION OF LINEAR MOMENTUM

Momentum is defined as the product of mass and velocity, where the mass is the total mass. It is a vector quantity, $\mathbf{p} = m\mathbf{v}$, with its direction the same as that of the velocity. In any interaction which is free from external influences it is observed that the vector sum of the momenta of the interacting bodies is conserved, or the components of momenta along the three linear coordinate axes are conserved in all three coordinates. The generality and power of the concept become evident when the momentum-conservation principle is found to be equally valid for elastic collisions in which energy is conserved and for inelastic collisions in which much of the incident kinetic energy is dissipated through friction or excitation.

As a simple illustration from classical physics consider the collision between particle $a$ in motion with velocity $v_a$ along the $x$ coordinate and particle $b$ at rest; particle $a$ is scattered at an angle $\theta$ in the $x$-$y$ plane and particle $b$ rebounds at angle $\phi$. The conservation of momentum in this process can be written

$$p_x = m_a v_a = m_a v_a' \cos \theta + m_b v_b' \cos \phi$$
$$p_y = 0 = m_a v_a' \sin \theta - m_b v_b' \sin \phi \tag{5.7}$$
$$p_z = 0$$

where the primes indicate velocities following the collision. We note that the angle $\phi$ is in the same plane as the angle $\theta$; the transverse components of momentum are equal and opposite. If the collision is elastic and energy is also conserved, there is the additional condition

$$\tfrac{1}{2}m_a v_a{}^2 = \tfrac{1}{2}m_a v_a'^2 + \tfrac{1}{2}m_b v_b'^2 \tag{5.8}$$

When this relation is included in solving the momentum equations, it is found that there is only one set of allowed values for $\theta$ and $\phi$.

The collision of billiard balls which is commonly used in mechanics texts to illustrate the conservation of momentum is not an ideal example since the directions of the rebounding balls after collision may be affected by their spins and by friction with the billiard table. However, it is still a useful visual example of the conservation of linear momentum in two dimensions (see Fig. 5.1).

For particles with velocities approaching that of light, relativistic formulations are required to specify their momenta. We have defined total energy $E = mc^2 = m_0 c^2 + T$, where $m_0$

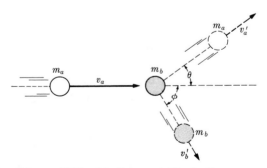

**Fig. 5.1** *Billiard ball impact illustrating conservation of energy,* $\tfrac{1}{2}m_a v_a{}^2 = \tfrac{1}{2}m_a v_a'^2 + \tfrac{1}{2}m_b v_b'^2$, *and momentum,* $m_a v_a = m_a v_a' \cos\theta + m_b v_b' \cos\phi$, $0 = m_a v_a' \sin\theta - m_b v_b' \sin\theta$.

is the rest mass and $T$ is the kinetic energy. Formally, the connection between total energy and momentum is expressed by the statement "the magnitude of the momentum four-vector is constant." This relation was derived from the definitions of special relativity as Eq. (3.20); it can also be written

$$E^2 = p^2c^2 + (m_0c^2)^2 \qquad\qquad (5.9)$$

Solving for the momentum

$$p = \frac{1}{c}[E^2 - (m_0c^2)^2]^{\frac{1}{2}} = \frac{1}{c}[T(T + 2m_0c^2)]^{\frac{1}{2}} \qquad (5.10)$$

The momentum is zero when the kinetic energy is zero, regardless of rest mass. For a particle with zero rest mass, such as the neutrino,

$$p = \frac{E}{c} \qquad\qquad (5.11)$$

Photons also have momentum. The momentum of a flux of light quanta manifests itself as radiation pressure and is assumed to be responsible for such macroscopic phenomena as the streaming of a comet's tail away from the sun. In particle physics, the individual photons entering or emerging from interactions are treated as particles with zero rest mass, velocity $c$, energy $E = h\nu$, and momentum $p = E/c$.

In the analysis of high-energy particle interactions the conservation of momentum is a powerful tool. Observation of the angles of emission of the product particles can be used to determine the momentum of an unknown product. Consider again the interaction $a + b \rightarrow c + d$, in which one of the product particles is unknown. The known incoming momentum of particle $a$ establishes a coordinate direction from which angles $\theta$ and $\phi$ are measured. In their simplest form the momentum relations are

$$p_a = p_c \cos \theta + p_d \cos \phi \qquad (5.12a)$$

$$0 = p_c \sin \theta - p_d \sin \phi \qquad (5.12b)$$

Measurement of both $\theta$ and $\phi$ will determine the momenta $p_c$ and $p_d$. Or, if one particle (say $d$) is not detected because of its being uncharged and nonionizing, measurement of both the angle $\theta$ and momentum $p_c$ of the observed particle will determine both the momentum $p_d$ and the angle $\phi$ of the neutral particle.

In order to determine the energy of an unknown particle more information is needed, specifically its mass. Then, if rest mass and momentum are both known, Eq. (5.9) can be used to determine its energy.

In the preceding section we discussed energy conservation and the requirement of a minimum "threshold" energy if the mass of the product particles exceeds that of the incident particles [see Eq. (5.4)]. The conservation of momentum puts another restriction on this threshold energy. Only a part of the incoming kinetic energy can be transformed into mass. Some energy of motion must remain to conserve momentum, and this amount of energy is not available to create additional mass. The momentum equations (5.12) and the energy equation (5.3) must be solved simultaneously to determine the threshold kinetic energy for production of a new, heavier particle. For example, when the bevatron at the University of California was designed, its energy of 6.0 GeV was chosen to exceed the threshold for production of proton-antiproton and neutron-antineutron pairs. With protons bombarding a high-$Z$ target, to create a nucleon-antinucleon pair (total rest-mass energy = 1.9 GeV), the threshold kinetic energy must be 5.4 GeV. In other words, the energy available for the creation of new or heavier particles is only a fraction of the incoming kinetic energy when the target is at rest.

To remove the above limitation, the technique has been proposed of storing circulating beams in magnetic *storage rings* in opposite directions and directing them into head-on collisions. For colliding particles having identical masses and energies, the total momentum in the laboratory is zero, and their total energy is available for excitation or production of new particles. Electron-positron colliding beam facilities are under construction at several laboratories, and a proton-proton storage ring is being constructed at CERN in Geneva.

A variety of instruments and experimental techniques are available to observe and to measure particle momentum. The most directly applicable technique is based on the motion of a charged particle in a magnetic field. A charged particle with charge-to-mass ratio $e/m$ moving at constant velocity $v$ in a direction transverse to a uniform magnetic field $B$ traverses a circular orbit of radius $r$. The momentum is given by

$$p = mv = eBr \qquad (5.13)$$

This relation for the momentum is valid for relativistic velocities as well as for low velocities. So measurement of the radius of curvature of a charged-particle trajectory in a magnetic field determines its momentum (see Fig. 5.2).

The cloud chamber and the liquid bubble chamber are particularly powerful tools. In a cloud chamber, ions formed along the particle trajectory in a supersaturated vapor are the condensation centers which produce a track of liquid droplets. In a bubble chamber a similar track of gas bubbles is formed in the liquid. If a magnetic field is superimposed on the chamber the tracks of the charged particles will be curved. The tracks are photographed stereoscopically and the photographs are analyzed to determine the radii of curvature in the magnetic field. Uncharged particles leave no tracks. If an ionizing track shows a sharp change in direction, it is presumed that an uncharged particle was formed in an interaction at this point. If an incident neutral particle has an interaction leading to two charged particles, the vertex of the V event shows the location, and the

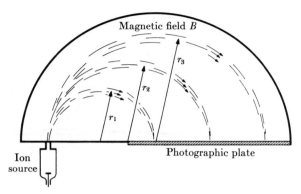

**Fig. 5.2**   *Illustration of deflection of several types of charged particles in circular orbits in a uniform transverse magnetic field B. Orbit radii are determined by particle momentum:* $r = \dfrac{m}{e}\dfrac{v}{B}$. *The focusing property of 180° deflection in a magnetic field is also illustrated.*

balance of transverse momenta identifies the incoming direction of the neutral particle (see Fig. 4.6).

Another technique which is useful in identifying particles is measurement of the ionization density along the track, which depends on particle velocity.   This density can be determined by measuring the number of developed grains per millimeter in the photographic record of the track.   Particles with velocities approaching that of light have the minimum density, and such "thin" tracks are generally those of light particles such as electrons. Slower particles have greater track densities and are usually the heavier particles such as baryons or mesons.   The relative ionization density as a function of particle energy is shown in Fig. 5.3 for electrons and for protons; the curve for mesons lies between these extremes.   The combination of a momentum measurement in a magnetic field with the grain density of the track usually provides a unique identification of any of the known particles.

The mass of an unknown particle produced in an interaction

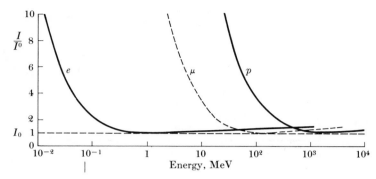

**Fig. 5.3**  *Relative ionization density as a function of kinetic energy for electrons, muons, and protons. Electrons of about 1-MeV energy, muons of about 200 MeV, and protons of 1000 MeV produce minimum ionization.*

can be determined by analysis of the momenta and energies of all of the particles. This analysis requires the use of relativistic formulations and three-dimensional geometry. The geometrical analysis is generally simpler if the laboratory observations are transformed into the coordinate system in which the center of mass (CM) of the particles entering or leaving the interaction is at rest. The techniques and coordinate transformation relations for such relativistic kinematic analyses are discussed in several textbooks.*

### CONSERVATION OF ANGULAR MOMENTUM

Another quality of matter which is conserved in any system free from external influences is the angular momentum of rotational motion. In classical physics, the combination of variables which defines the conserved quantity is $mvr$, the product of the linear momentum $mv$ and the distance $r$ to the axis of rotation. The principle of conservation of angular momentum was first

* *M. L. Goldberger and K. M. Watson, "Collision Theory," Wiley, New York, 1964.*

recognized in and applied to the rotational motion of mechanical systems. Many simple and familiar examples exist, in which friction and other dissipative influences are small enough to allow direct observation and measurement of the angular momentum. For example, a small object of mass $m$ which is swung in a circle on a string of length $r$ and which has instantaneous linear velocity $v$ has angular momentum $mvr$. A lightweight wheel with a heavy mass $m$ distributed uniformly around the rim at radius $r$, which is rotating on its axis with a rim velocity $v$, also has angular momentum $mvr$ (see Fig. 5.4).

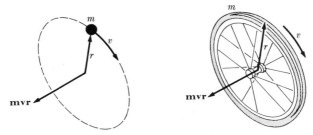

**Fig. 5.4**   *Angular momentum* **mvr** *for a ball on a string, or for a bicycle wheel, is illustrated by a vector along the axis of rotation.*

Angular momentum is an *axial vector* quantity, unlike linear momentum which is a *polar vector*. The direction of the vector is chosen (by convention) to be along the axis of rotation and pointing in the direction of advance of a right-hand screw. It can be illustrated graphically by an arrow plotted along the axis of rotation in the defined direction which has a length proportional to its magnitude. Both the magnitude and the direction are given by the vector cross product of $m\mathbf{v}$ and $\mathbf{r}$, where $m\mathbf{v}$ is the vector linear momentum and $\mathbf{r}$ is the radius vector from the axis to the location of the mass. We will use the symbol $\mathbf{S}$ for this vector angular momentum

$$\mathbf{S} = m\mathbf{v} \times \mathbf{r} \tag{5.14}$$

Angular momentum exists for objects of any shape and for motion about any axis. For rigid objects the rotational frequency is the same for all parts of the object. For any small part of the mass $dm$ at radius $r$ which has linear velocity $v$, the frequency is $f = v/2\pi r$, and the increment of the angular momentum $\mathbf{dS}$ for this mass $dm$ is $\mathbf{dS} = dm\,\mathbf{vr} = 2\pi f r^2\,dm$. The angular momentum for the entire object can be obtained by integrating over the mass of the object

$$\mathbf{S} = 2\pi f \int^{m} \mathbf{r}^2\,dm = 2\pi f I \qquad (5.15)$$

where the integral $I = \int^{m} \mathbf{r}^2\,dm$ is the moment of inertia.

Objects of the same mass but of different shapes can have widely different moments of inertia. A decrease in radius of some portion of a spinning body will reduce its moment of inertia. If this change in shape is accomplished by internal forces the rotational frequency will change to keep the angular momentum constant. For example, if an ice skater spinning on the toe of one skate starts his spin with arms extended, he can speed up his spin dramatically by pulling in his arms. The orbits of the planets are ellipses with the center of mass of the sun and planet at one focus. As a direct consequence of the conservation of angular momentum, the linear velocity varies with the radial distance from the sun, being higher when the planet is close and lower when it is farther removed. This fact is expressed quantitatively in Kepler's laws of planetary motion. The direction of an angular-momentum vector also remains constant unless changed by some external force or torque. This property is utilized in the gyroscopic compass, which maintains its direction in space if it is supported on friction-free bearings and gimbals, regardless of changes in course of the ship or aircraft on which it is mounted.

Angular momentum can also be defined for a system of two or more bodies, as the vector sum of their separate angular momenta about a common axis such as one through the center of mass of the system.  If some of the separate angular momenta are clockwise about this axis and others are counterclockwise, they tend to cancel.  In the case of two identical objects in counterrotation about the same axis with the same angular frequencies and the same moments of inertia, the total angular momentum is zero.  Angular momentum can be transferred or exchanged between two objects within a system if they collide or interact.  For example, if two skaters on opposing courses touch hands as they pass, they will both be set into rotation with equal and opposite angular momenta about an axis through the point of contact.

In the mechanical world it is difficult to devise a moving system which is completely free from extraneous influences or forces.  The smaller the dissipative forces the closer the system approaches perpetual motion, but it can never be achieved. The dissipative forces must be considered in the total balance of energy.  Similarly, in mechanical systems, external torques can change the angular momentum.  Spinning gyroscopes can run down due to torques applied through friction in the bearings or in the air.  The more nearly isolated the system can be made, the more closely does its angular momentum remain constant.  Our conclusion that angular momentum is absolutely conserved is based on a long sequence of experimental studies and observations of increasing precision.  With experience, this conservation principle has become as solidly based as any of the laws of motion.

### ANGULAR MOMENTUM OF PARTICLES

Angular momentum is also conserved in the motions of the particles constituting an atom.  The intrinsic spin of a single particle about its own axis is one type of angular momentum; another type is the orbital motion of the electron around the nucleus.  In a complex atom many electrons are involved, and the total angular momentum of the atom is the vector sum of all the spins and orbital motions.  The limitations placed on these motions by the basic postulates of the quantum theory and the wave mechanics have no counterpart in the classical description of rotational motion. In the atomic system there are no frictional or dissipative forces. The electron cannot be considered a point charge or even a sphere of very small size; the position of an electron within an atom can be roughly localized only within a distance of the order of its associated wavelength. However, the assignment of quantized values of intrinsic spin to the electron and to the angular momentum of its orbital motion has led to a theory which is completely successful in correlating and calculating the known experimental facts about the atom. The postulates of quantum mechanics have been formulated to preserve the validity of the conservation of angular momentum in atomic systems. It is truly remarkable that this property of motion called angular momentum can play such a fundamental role in atomic physics as well as in classical mechanics. It justifies our conclusion that angular momentum is a fundamental quality of matter and that its conservation is a basic attribute of nature.

The intrinsic spin $s$ of an elementary particle is measured in units of $h/2\pi$, where $h$ is Planck's constant. According to general quantum-mechanical principles, spin can have only integral or half-integral values. This is the basic natural unit for angular momentum and is the "quantum" of quantum mechanics. The existence of this natural unit shows that angular momentum is an extraordinarily basic concept. There is no equivalent natural unit for other qualities such as mass, length, or time, so far as we know. These intrinsic spins exist both when the particles are in the free state and when they are bound in atoms.

In an atomic orbit another postulate of quantum mechanics leads to the requirement that the electron spin must be aligned with the orbital spin. Following the Pauli exclusion principle, only two allowed states exist with the electron spin either parallel or antiparallel to the orbital angular momentum, and only two electrons can occupy this energy state with $s = \frac{1}{2}$ and $-\frac{1}{2}$.

The angular momentum of orbital motion, $l$, is also quantized in units of $h/2\pi$ and can have only integral numbers of such units, depending on the allowed energy states and the degree of eccentricity of the orbit. This survey is not the place for a more detailed discussion of atomic structure. We note here only a few general conclusions. Except for the ferromagnetic atoms or for the odd electrons in those atoms with odd atomic number, the electron spins are paired and cancel. In general, most of the orbital spins also are paired and tend to cancel. The total angular momentum $j$, which is the vector sum of $l$ and $s$ over all the electrons, is itself quantized with a small number of quantum units. In atomic physics angular momentum is a "good" quantum number and is conserved in all atomic transitions.

A spinning electric charge produces a magnetic field, and each charged particle which has spin has a definite magnetic moment as though it were a small magnet. The spinning electron has a magnetic moment $\mu_e$ called the Bohr magneton

$$\mu_e = \frac{eh}{4\pi m_0 c} = 9.273 \times 10^{-28} \text{ joule/gauss} \qquad (5.16)$$

In a magnetic field $B$ the spin is lined up with the field. The amount of energy required to flip the spin direction opposite the field is $2\mu_e B$; if the electron spin flips back, a photon of this

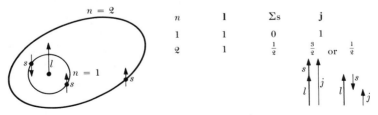

**Fig. 5.5**  *Pictorial representation of spins in a three-electron atom. The unpaired electron in the $n = 2$ orbit with $l = 1$ can be oriented with its spin either parallel or antiparallel to $l$, for a total angular momentum $j$ of $\frac{3}{2}$ or $\frac{1}{2}$.*

energy is emitted. For example, with $B = 1000$ gauss, the radiation emitted has a frequency of about 3000 megacycles ($10^{-5}$ eV), which is in the microwave region. If a radiofrequency coil surrounding a sample containing electrons which are aligned in a field is tuned through this frequency, energy will be absorbed from the radiofrequency field in a narrow band at this resonant frequency. This phenomenon can also be used to measure the magnetic field intensity with high precision.

The magnetic moment of a spinning proton is given in terms of the *nuclear magneton*, which is $\frac{1}{1836}$ of a Bohr magneton, since the nuclear magneton contains the proton mass instead of the electron mass. The proton magnetic moment has been measured to be $\mu_p = 2.7934$ nuclear magnetons $\simeq 1.5 \times 10^{-3}$ Bohr magnetons. Strangely enough, although the neutron has no electric charge, it does have a magnetic moment, oriented in the opposite direction and so defined as negative: $\mu_n = -1.9135$ nuclear magnetons. Unpaired protons or neutrons in a sample placed in a magnetic field will also absorb radiofrequency energy to flip their spins at the resonant frequencies determined by the magnetic field. The technique of nuclear magnetic resonance is also used in flux meters to obtain precise calibrations of high-intensity magnetic fields.

In nuclear physics, the concepts of angular momentum and intrinsic spin are taken over directly from atomic physics. After years of experimental and theoretical study, it is now known that the same postulates of quantum mechanics apply as for the atom. The protons and neutrons which compose the nucleus each have intrinsic spin $s = \frac{1}{2}$ and obey the Pauli principle. Two protons and two neutrons can exist in the lowest quantized energy state in a nucleus which "explains" the unusual stability and small mass of the $He^4$ nucleus. In heavier nuclei the additional protons and neutrons occupy higher-energy states and are paired in each. This leads to the *shell structure* of nuclei and the relative stability in nuclear interactions of those nuclei with closed shells. The total angular momentum $I$ of the nucleus is the vector sum of the intrinsic spins and of the orbital angular momenta of the individual nucleons about the center of mass. This total angular momentum of a nucleus is itself quantized, having a small number of integral or half-integral units of $h/2\pi$. Closed-shell nuclei in general have zero total spin. The rapid advance in understanding of nuclear physics and the properties of nuclei has come largely from this application of quantum mechanical principles developed for atomic physics, which include the conservation of angular momentum.

Angular momentum is conserved in all interactions between high-energy particles. Only two types of angular momentum are involved. Each incident or product particle has its own intrinsic spin, and the orientation of these spins must be considered in the vector sum of angular momenta. Particles can also have orbital angular momentum $l$ due to their relative motion about a common axis. This relative orbital motion is analogous to the example cited above of two skaters on opposing courses who touch hands as they pass. With particles, the orbital angular momentum can be represented by a vector perpendicular to the plane established by the recoiling particles. In such interactions the vector sum of both types of angular momentum, $\mathbf{j} = \mathbf{s} + \mathbf{l}$, is the quantity which is conserved.

The elementary particles can be grouped into classes with different values of intrinsic spin, zero, half-integral, or integral, in units of $h/2\pi$. The number of possible alternative orientations of spin (spin states) depends on the value of the spin quantum number. A particle with spin 0 (i. e., mesons) has only one state, that of 0. Particles with spin $\frac{1}{2}$ (fermions) have two states, $+\frac{1}{2}$ and $-\frac{1}{2}$, depending on the orientation parallel or antiparallel to the chosen spin axis. Particles with spin 1 (photons and heavy mesons) can have three states, $+1$, 0, and $-1$. In general, a particle can be produced in any one of its allowed spin states, and with equal probability, as long as the total vector angular momentum is conserved. The interaction probability (cross section) involves a summation over all allowed

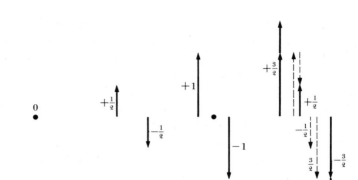

**Fig. 5.6** *Allowed vector orientations for particle spins of 0, $\frac{1}{2}$, 1, and $\frac{3}{2}$.*

spin states of the product particles. If competing interactions with different sets of products can occur, their relative cross sections are determined by the number of allowed spin states. Consequently, rather imprecise data on relative total cross sections of competing reactions will allow the spin of an unknown product particle to be determined.

The spin, the number of spin states, and any relative orbital angular momentum enter in determining the angular distributions of the products of a particular interaction. The cross sections in the forward, backward, and transverse directions in center-of-mass space, and so the angular distributions observed in the laboratory, are determined by these spins and angular momenta. A full discussion of this subject goes beyond the scope of this survey. For present purposes, it is sufficient to note that spin assignments can often be made or confirmed through analyses of the angular distributions observed in experiments.

When the particles in an interaction are initially at rest relative to one another, orbital angular momentum is not involved, and the total angular momentum is just the vector sum of their spins. An example is the process in which a positron is slowed down sufficiently to combine with an electron, and the total mass energy is released in the form of photons

$$e^+ + e^- \rightarrow \gamma + \gamma \quad \text{or} \quad \rightarrow \gamma + \gamma + \gamma \qquad (5.17)$$

The positron and electron each have $s = \frac{1}{2}$ and, depending on their relative spin orientations, the total angular momentum can be either 0 or 1. Each of the product photons has a spin $s = 1$, and at least two must be emitted if linear momentum is to be conserved in their recoil. If electron spins are opposed so the total angular momentum is 0, two photons recoiling in opposite directions with spin vectors also opposed will conserve angular momentum.

However, if the electron spins are parallel so that the total angular momentum is 1, the vector sum of the photon spins must equal 1; under certain conditions, three photons can be emitted. When the positron and electron first approach each other they can form, temporarily, an "atom" in which the positron takes the place of a nucleus. In this *positronium atom* the two particles have the same mass, so they revolve about their common center of mass. The positronium atom can survive for a time sufficient for its properties to be studied in the laboratory. Relative motion of the two particles exists in this atom, and the complete quantum-mechanical analysis of the annihilation processes into either two or three photons must include their orbital angular momenta. The three-photon process is observed experimentally in only about 0.1 percent of the processes where $(e^+ e^-)$ annihilation occurs.

When a single particle, at rest or in flight, decays into two product particles, orbital motion is not involved. For example, in the decay of a pion into a muon and a neutrino, $\pi^\pm \rightarrow \mu^\pm + \nu$ [see Eqs. (4.7) and (4.8)], the spin of the pion is 0. The muon and neutrino, both of which have spin $s = \frac{1}{2}$, must be emitted in opposite directions to conserve linear momentum and with opposite orientations of their spins to conserve angular momentum.

However, if a single particle decays into three products, one of them may have angular motion relative to the others, and its orbital angular momentum must be considered in the total momentum balance. This feature is involved in the beta decay processes in which parity conservation is violated, discussed in Chap. 7.

## CONSERVATION OF CHARGE

All experimental evidence shows that electric charge is conserved. In any closed system or any system which is electrically isolated, the net charge is a constant. Electric charge is assumed to be a unique and fundamental property of matter in our theory of electromagnetism. However, no theory has yet been able to explain the origin of electric charge or why it exists. The modern quantum electrodynamics has removed some of the inconsistencies of earlier theories of electromagnetism, but it has nothing to say about the origin of charge.

The unit of charge is the charge of an electron, which by long-accepted convention is considered negative. In terms of the standard engineering units, $q = -1.60207 \times 10^{-19}$ coul. The charge on the proton is identical in magnitude and is positive. The charge of neutral particles or neutral atoms is identically zero. When electrons are separated from neutral atoms or molecules, by friction or by other means, the magnitude of the negative charge removed is always equal to the positive charge left behind. Experimental tests to determine whether the electron does decay have given negative results and establish the electron lifetime as greater than $10^{19}$ years. Other experiments show that the magnitudes of the electron and proton charge cannot differ by more than 1 part in $10^{20}$. Charge conservation must be regarded as thoroughly verified.

Particle physics has introduced a corollary into the definition of charge conservation. In the creation of particles out of energy, if one is charged the other has the opposite charge. Electron-positron pairs can be produced by photons (in the presence of a nuclear field in which momentum can be conserved) if the photon energy is greater than the masses of the created particles (1.02 MeV). The positron is an antiparticle; when it is sufficiently slowed down by ionizing collisions it will annihilate with the first electron it encounters, releasing the total mass energy of the pair as uncharged photons. So the net charge in the system remains the same in creation or annihilation processes. The same applies to the creation of heavy particle-antiparticle pairs. In the annihilation of a negative proton (antiproton) with a positive proton, some of the available mass energy (1876 MeV) usually appears in the form of charged and neutral pions or other particles; in all cases observed, the net charge of all the charged products is zero.

Charge conservation is utilized in the analysis of experimental data. Take, for example, a liquid-hydrogen bubble chamber exposed to a flux of high-energy photons. Single charged particle tracks originating in the chamber are observed only in those cases where the range of the second charged particle (i.e., the recoil ion) is too short to produce observable ionization. Most of the observed tracks are electron-positron pairs created from the energy of the photons. Three-prong stars consist of a recoil proton from the hydrogen in the chamber and a pair of charged particles such as pions; in this case the residual electron from the hydrogen atom does not participate in the interaction and is left behind with insufficient energy to produce ionization. Still more complex events can occur if the available energy is sufficient. For example, five-prong stars consisting of a recoil proton and two charged pairs are observed. Each pair is a particle and antiparticle, and their charges have opposite sign.

Some of the more recent predictions based on group theory postulate particle states with fractional electronic charge called *quarks* (see Chap. 12). However, there is as yet no experimental evidence to confirm such predictions. This remains a subject of very great interest, however, since there is no theoretical "proof" that charge must always exist in units of the electronic charge. If particles with fractional electronic charge were to be observed, the assumption is that other particles with fractional charge would be produced, and that charge would still be conserved.

## CONSERVATION OF PARTICLE NUMBER

Particle physics has added another basic conservation principle, that of the conservation of total number in certain classes of particles. This principle was not required or formally recognized during the classical era of science, but it is as broad and general in its application as the four classical conservation laws. It applies to the two classes, baryons and leptons, which are fermions with intrinsic spin $\frac{1}{2}$ and which include the three components of atoms, the proton, neutron, and electron. On the other hand, particle number is not conserved in the two classes of bosons (mesons and photons) which have intrinsic spins of 0 or 1.

Baryons include nucleons ($n$ and $p$) and hyperons, a name given to strongly interacting fermions with mass values greater than for nucleons and whose final decay products include one nucleon. The term hyperon was used for a time before the symmetry of baryons was clearly recognized. It is no longer needed or used except to distinguish the heavier particles from nucleons.

The hyperons are the heavy members of the strange particle pairs produced in associated production and include four groups of increasing mass: lambda ($\Lambda$), sigma ($\Sigma$), xi ($\Xi$), and omega ($\Omega$). They differ from each other in features other than their mass values, specifically in the number of charge states. This property is discussed further in Chap. 8. A common characteristic of hyperons is that their production interactions involve the strong nuclear force.

Like other fermions, baryons can be created from energy only in particle-antiparticle pairs. We define the baryon number

of a baryon as $+1$ for a particle and $-1$ for an antiparticle.
For all other particles the baryon number is 0. The symbol
normally used is the same as that used for atomic number $(A)$.
The conservation principle states that in any interaction the
baryon number is the same before and after the interaction.
Consider, for example, the process by which antiprotons were
first produced in an accelerator, at the University of California

$$p + p \rightarrow p + p + p + \overline{p^-} \tag{5.18}$$

Another example is the process by which the antiproton annihi-
lates with a normal proton; a typical annihilation might result
in the products

$$\overline{p^-} + p \rightarrow x\pi^+ + x\pi^- + y\pi^0 \tag{5.19}$$

The total rest mass of both protons is transformed into $(2x + y)$
pions plus their kinetic energies with no baryon products.

Baryon number is intimately associated with other quantum
numbers of the strange particles involved in strong interactions,
such as isotopic spin and strangeness. This relationship will
be explored further in the following chapters. The selection
rule which describes the conservation of baryon number is
fundamental in defining the range of validity of strong interactions. It describes our observation that the proton is stable
and does not decay into positrons or muons; for example, it
forbids the reaction $p \nrightarrow e^+ + \pi^0$, even though it is allowed by
other conservation laws.

Lepton number $(L)$ is also conserved. Leptons (which are
also fermions) are created only in particle-antiparticle pairs and
annihilate only in pairs. Lepton number is defined as $+1$ for particles, $-1$ for antiparticles, and 0 for all other classes of particles.
Leptons include the *electron family* of $e^-$, $\overline{e^+}$, $\nu_e$, and $\overline{\nu_e}$, and the
*muon family* of $\mu^-$, $\overline{\mu^+}$, $\nu_\mu$, and $\overline{\nu_\mu}$. Conservation of number also
holds within each of these families. In each family the negatively

charged member is the particle and the positively charged is the antiparticle.  If a particle of either family is produced in an interaction, another product must be an antiparticle of the same family.  An example is the beta decay of the neutron

$$n \to p + e^- + \overline{\nu_e} \qquad\qquad (5.20)$$

in which the products include two electron-family members. Charged muons are created in the pion decay processes

$$\pi^+ \to \overline{\mu^+} + \nu_\mu \qquad \text{and} \qquad \pi^- \to \mu^- + \overline{\nu_\mu} \qquad (5.21)$$

in which muon family number is conserved.  The muons decay into three particles, including two electron family members

$$\overline{\mu^+} \to \overline{e^+} + \nu_e + \nu_\mu \qquad \text{and} \qquad \mu^- \to e^- + \overline{\nu_e} + \nu_\mu \qquad (5.22)$$

Electron-family number and muon-family number are conserved as well as total lepton number in each of these examples.

Before the discovery of the muon neutrino it was believed that electrons and muons formed a single family and that only total lepton number was conserved.  The process $\mu^- \nrightarrow e^- + \gamma$ would have satisfied all the classical conservation laws and lepton number conservation.  However, it has not been observed experimentally even in a single example.  When muon neutrinos were observed to be different from electron neutrinos and the conservation requirement for both electron and muon families was recognized, this puzzle was resolved.

The role of conservation laws is to describe what does happen and to explain why unseen events do not happen.  The five conservation laws discussed in this chapter are valid for all types of interactions and in all physical phenomena.  There are no known exceptions which violate any one of them.  Despite the seemingly arbitrary definitions of the qualities of matter which they describe, or of formalisms such as that which utilizes negative numbers to extend the family number conservation laws to antiparticles, these conservation laws correlate and explain a broad and diversified range of physical phenomena. When we find such widespread consistency we are justified in assuming that these laws represent basic attributes of nature. Whether our choice of these particular qualities of matter is unique, whether simpler and more inclusive conservation laws can be found, or whether some more fundamental method of correlating observations is possible, are questions for the future. A more general approach to conservation laws through basic symmetry principles is discussed in Chap. 12.

Still other qualities of matter have been identified for which other conservation laws can be formulated, but which have a more limited jurisdiction. These qualities are conserved for some types of particle interactions but not for others. The conservation principles for strangeness, for isotopic spin, and for parity that have evolved in the study of particle physics are of this type. They will be described and their limitations discussed in the following chapters.

# chapter 6

# MASSES
# OF THE
# OBSERVABLE
# PARTICLES

THE MOST IMPORTANT IDENTIFYING CHARACTERISTIC of a particle is its rest mass. Mass is a form of energy, following Einstein's equivalence relation $E = mc^2$. The masses of the particles listed in Tables 1 and 2 are given in MeV units. One MeV is the kinetic energy acquired by a particle carrying a single electronic charge in falling through a potential difference of $10^6$ volts. The conversion factors between mass and energy are

$$1 \text{ g} = 8.9879 \times 10^{13} \text{ joules} = 5.612 \times 10^{26} \text{ MeV}$$

or

$$1 \text{ MeV} = 1.60207 \times 10^{-13} \text{ joule} = 1.7825 \times 10^{-27} \text{ g}*$$

In nuclear physics the masses of atoms are commonly expressed in atomic mass units (amu)(see Chap. 5). It can be shown that 1 amu = 931.16 MeV.* In particle physics we deal with single particles regardless of charge, rather than with neutral atoms as in nuclear physics. Particle masses are expressed directly in MeV units.

## ELECTRONS

The electron is the lightest particle which has mass; it carries a unit electric charge and is one of the stable constituents of atoms. As such its mass must be considered a fundamental constant of nature. However, there is no theoretical explanation why the electron has its specific value of mass. Quantum electrodynamics, which explains and predicts essentially all observed

---

* *Values derived from J. W. M. Dumond and E. R. Cohen, Rev. Mod. Phys.*, **25**: *691 (1953).*

atomic phenomena, has nothing to say about the origin of the mass of the electron. Some speculative thought associates the electron mass with the unit charge, but no formula exists for calculating mass from charge, and there is still no solid theoretical basis for this assumption. This remains a problem for the future. We must depend on experimental measurements for the value of the electron mass.

Electron mass is determined from independent measurements of the charge-to-mass ratio $e/m$ and the charge $e$. Experiments on the deflection of electron beams by electric and magnetic fields can provide values of $e/m$ but not for $e$ or $m$ separately. Analyses of atomic spectra with ruled gratings, combined with basic atomic theory, also give values of $e/m$ for the electron. Electrochemical studies of the amount of charge required to dissociate a gram atom of a univalent molecule in solution (the faraday), combined with the number of atoms in a gram atom (Avogadro's number), give an approximate value for the electron charge. The Millikan oil-drop experiment gives an independent measurement of $e$, but it is dependent on the measured value of the viscosity of air. When all these values are correlated and weighted by the experimental errors involved, a "best value" of electron mass is obtained, which is

$$m_0 \text{ (electron)} = 0.9107 \times 10^{-27} \text{ g} = 0.51098 \text{ MeV}$$

The mass value above is the rest mass for an electron with zero or very low energy. For electrons of relativistic energies the mass is given by $m = m_0/(1 - v^2/c^2)^{\frac{1}{2}}$.

The positron is the antielectron. Theoretically, an antiparticle should have a mass identical with that of the particle. A few deflection experiments of relatively low accuracy confirm this assumption; the mass-energy balance in both production and annihilation processes with positrons is also in agreement. In the absence of any evidence to the contrary, we accept the validity of the theoretical prediction and assign the same mass.

## PROTONS

The proton is the other stable component of atoms. Knowledge of the proton mass, another basic constant of nature, is essential in atomic and nuclear physics. It has been measured in a variety of experiments on the deflection of hydrogen-ion beams in electric and magnetic fields (see Chap. 2) and also by analyses of experimental results from nuclear disintegrations. Improvements in the values of the several fundamental constants which are involved in the experiments have, in recent years, brought these results into reasonable agreement.

The results of mass-spectroscopic measurements have been summarized from time to time to deduce by least-squares analysis the best values of atomic masses. The doublet method (see Chap. 2) forms the basis for tables of atomic masses in which the uncertainties are a few parts per million. The best value of the $H^1$ mass in the recent literature is

$$H^1 = 1.008146 \pm 0.000003 \text{ amu}*$$

From this, by subtracting the mass of the electron and converting to MeV units, we obtain for the mass of the proton,

$$m_p \text{ (proton)} = 938.21 \text{ MeV}$$

In theoretical calculations in atomic or nuclear physics the mass of the electron $m_0$ is occasionally used as a basic mass unit. In this system of units the proton mass is $m_p = 1836.1 \ m_0$. However, in experimental high-energy physics the proton mass is most commonly expressed in MeV units.

In principle, the mass of any charged particle can be determined through similar measurements utilizing the deflections in electric and magnetic fields. In practice it is more difficult because of the low intensities and the short lifetimes of the particles produced in high-energy interactions. In some cases alternate techniques of much lower precision have been used, such as

* *See R. D. Evans, "The Atomic Nucleus," McGraw-Hill, New York, 1955.*

observations of the ranges and ionization densities of particle tracks in photographic emulsions or in bubble chambers. Still different techniques are required to determine the mass of neutral particles. Typical methods are the study of the charged decay products from neutral particles or measurements of the angles and momenta of charged particles recoiling in scattering collisions.

### NEUTRONS

The neutron mass has been determined from nuclear disintegration reactions. First it was necessary to verify the mass-energy balance in nuclear reactions through studies of a variety of nuclear disintegrations in which the observed energy change $Q$ could be correlated with the change in mass. The agreement justifies the conclusion that mass plus energy are quantitatively conserved and that the atoms formed by nuclear reactions are identical with their stable sister atoms. In a nuclear disintegration such as $a + b \rightarrow c + d$, from which the $Q$ value is obtained from the outgoing and incoming kinetic energies [see Chap. 5, Eq. (5.1)], the mass difference of particles $a$ and $c$, for example, is

$$(m_a - m_c) = (m_d - m_b) - Q \qquad (6.1)$$

The mass difference $(n - \mathrm{H}^1)$ can be evaluated from several independent cycles of nuclear interactions. The most direct and accurate determination* comes from the measured threshold energy (negative $Q$ value) of the reaction

$$\mathrm{H}^1 + \mathrm{H}^3 \rightarrow n + \mathrm{He}^3 + Q \qquad Q = -0.764 \text{ MeV} \qquad (6.2)$$

It is known from other nuclear disintegration results that $\mathrm{H}^3 - \mathrm{He}^3 = +0.018$ MeV. The best value of the neutron-hydrogen mass difference obtained from these numbers is $n - \mathrm{H}^1 = 0.782$ MeV. The mass of $\mathrm{H}^1$ includes the atomic

* R. D. Evans, *"The Atomic Nucleus,"* p. 131, McGraw-Hill, New York, 1955.

electron.  When the proton mass is used, we obtain

$$n - m_p = 1.294 \text{ MeV}$$

from which the neutron mass is found to be

$$m_n \text{ (neutron)} = 939.50 \text{ MeV}$$

### MUONS

The first estimate of the mass of the muon* came from studies of the ionization density of the tracks of mesonic particles in cloud chamber photographs of cosmic rays (see Chaps. 4 and 5).

When accelerator sources of pions and muons became available, it was possible to determine their masses with better accuracy from the observed particle energies in their decay processes.  When slowed down, the positive pions were observed to decay into muons.  The muons decay into positrons which have a continuous spectrum of energies indicating a three-body decay

$$\mu^+ \rightarrow e^+ + \nu_e + \nu_\mu + 105 \text{ MeV} \qquad (6.3)$$

The momenta of the charged particles were observed through the curvature of their tracks in cloud chambers with superimposed magnetic fields (see Fig. 4.5).  Assuming conservation of momentum, the extrapolated maximum energy of the positron spectrum (both neutrinos recoiling in the opposite direction) provides a measure of the mass of the muon.

In recent years a more precise value of mass has been obtained from measurements of the magnetic moment of the muon $\mu_\mu$.  The magnetic moments of electrons $\mu_e$ and protons $\mu_p$ are basic constants in atomic and nuclear physics and have

---

* *Previously called the $\mu$ meson.  It is now known to be a lepton rather than a strongly interacting meson, and we use the more specific name muon.*

been measured with high accuracy. The gyromagnetic ratio $g$ (ratio of the magnetic dipole moment to the spin angular momentum) is also a basic constant of atomic particles and is known to high accuracy for protons and electrons. The relationship between these quantities involves the mass of the particle; ratios for different particles give ratios of masses, such as

$$\frac{\mu_e}{\mu_\mu} = \frac{g_e}{g_\mu} \frac{m_\mu}{m_e} \tag{6.4}$$

What was actually measured was the gyromagnetic ratio of the muons in a beam coming from an accelerator by observing the angular velocity of precession of the magnetic moment in a magnetic field. The ratio of magnetic moments of the muon and the proton was also measured which, combined with the electron-proton ratio, gave the electron-muon ratio. Combination of these values of the ratios of moments and $g$ factors in Eq. (6.4) gives a value for the mass of the muon of

$$m \text{ (muon)} = 105.65 \text{ MeV}$$

This value is presumed to be the same for both positive and negative muons.

### PIONS

As indicated in the previous section, the charged pion decays at rest into a muon and a neutrino (in the absence of matter)

$$\pi^+ \rightarrow \mu^+ + \nu_\mu + 34 \text{ MeV} \tag{6.5}$$

The $\pi^+$ pion can be brought to rest (actually to thermal velocities) by collisions in matter, such as in a cloud-chamber gas or a bubble-chamber liquid, and the momentum of the product $\mu^+$ muon can be measured by the curvature of its track in a magnetic field; the neutrino also emitted must have equal and opposite momentum. Assuming the neutrino to have zero rest mass, the energy release in the decay process can be computed and the pion mass determined

$$m_{\pi^+} \text{ (charged pion)} = 139.7 \text{ MeV}$$

Direct observation of the decay process of the $\pi^-$ pion at rest is handicapped by the formation of $\pi^-$ mesic atoms, in which the pion enters an atomic Bohr orbit from which it can be captured by a nuclear proton in a charge-exchange process. However, a few measurements of the ratio of masses through range measurements of $\pi^-$ and $\pi^+$ pions in flight confirm the assumption that the $\pi^-$ pion has the same mass as the $\pi^+$ pion.

Other methods of determining the pion mass are based on studies of the ranges and ionization densities of charged particle tracks in photographic emulsions, which can be analyzed to give mass ratios of $m_{\pi^+}/m_p$ and $m_{\pi^-}/m_p$. The results of all these measurements are consistent with the value cited above. The consistency of the results from the several methods justifies the assumption of zero mass for the $\mu$ neutrino also emitted in the decay process.

The neutral pion $\pi^0$ can be formed through the charge-exchange process

$$\pi^- + p \rightarrow n + \pi^0 \tag{6.6}$$

following capture of the $\pi^-$ in a Bohr orbit (i.e., in liquid hydrogen). The $\pi^0$ decays promptly ($10^{-16}$ sec) into two photons (see Fig. 4.5).

$$\pi^0 \rightarrow \gamma + \gamma \tag{6.7}$$

A competing reaction is the capture process

$$\pi^- + p \rightarrow n + \gamma \tag{6.8}$$

In both cases photons and neutrons are the observable products. However, the neutrons from the two reactions have different energies, since the $\pi^0$ has a finite rest mass, and are emitted with different velocities. The neutrons require a finite time (about $10^{-7}$ sec) to travel to a neutron detector located a few meters from the target, and the two groups of neutrons can be observed in delayed coincidences with a photon detector placed close to and on the opposite side of the target (see Fig. 6.1) corresponding

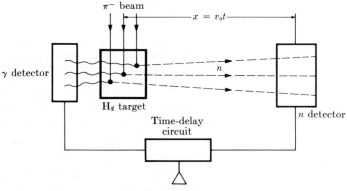

**Fig. 6.1** *Schematic experimental arrangement for time-of-flight determination of the mass of the $\pi^0$ pion in the reaction $\pi^- + p \rightarrow n + \pi^0$.*

to different flight times and different velocities. The slower group is from the $\pi^0$ process. From the measured neutron velocities and the kinematics of the two interactions, it is possible to obtain a value for the mass of the pion

$$m_{\pi^0} \text{ (neutral pion)} = 134.99 \text{ MeV}$$

An independent measurement, obtained earlier, from studies of the angles of emission of the two photons from the $\pi^0$ decay in flight [Eq. (6.7)] is in agreement with the value above. In the frame of reference of the moving particle, momentum conservation requires that the two photons have equal and opposite momenta. In the laboratory frame of reference, in which the $\pi^0$ has forward momentum, the two photons emerge in the forward direction with an opening angle between them which is a function of their momenta. Relativistic analysis of this process allows both the momentum and velocity of the $\pi^0$ to be determined, from which the mass is obtained. We note that the neutral pion has a smaller mass than the charged pions, by about 4.6 MeV.

### KAONS

The $K$ particle, or kaon, is known to have a variety of decay modes, as shown in Table 2. One of these observed modes, $K^+ \rightarrow \pi^+ + \pi^- + \pi^+$, shows that the kaon mass must be greater than three times the mass of the charged pion. The kinetic energies of the three charged-pion products can be determined, either through their range in photographic emulsions or through the curvature of their tracks in a bubble chamber in a magnetic field. Another decay mode is into two pions: $K^+ \rightarrow \pi^+ + \pi^0$. Conservation of momentum is assumed to determine the direction of emission and momentum of the $\pi^0$. From kinematic analyses of these decay processes, the mass of the positively charged kaon $K^+$ is found to be

$$m_{K^+} \text{ (positive kaon)} = 493.8 \text{ MeV}$$

and is assumed to be the same for $K^-$.

Two methods have been used to determine the mass of the neutral kaon $(K^0)$ or of its antiparticle $(\overline{K^0})$. One method is similar to that employed for the neutral pion, involving the production reaction $K^- + p \rightarrow \overline{K^0} + n$, and using time-of-flight measurements to determine the neutron velocity. The analysis is more complicated because the $K^-$ kaons are captured not from Bohr orbits but in flight, and their incident momenta must be included in the analysis. In a second method, the momentum of the $\overline{K^0}$ is determined from the momenta of its charged decay products in the reaction $K^0 \rightarrow \pi^+ + \pi^-$ from the angles of emission and curvatures of the pion tracks in a magnetic field. The results of both methods show a mass difference between the $\overline{K^0}$ and the $K^-$ of 4.0 MeV, with the neutral particle being heavier.

Another procedure believed to measure the same quantity ($\overline{K^0} - K^-$ difference) is based on the kinematic analysis of the two production reactions $\pi^- + p \rightarrow \Sigma^- + K^+$ and $\pi^- + p \rightarrow \Lambda^0 + K^0$. Taking the (independently) measured values for the masses of the $\Sigma^-$ and $\Lambda^0$ particles (as given in the following section), the mass difference ($K^0 - K^+$) can be obtained; it has the same value of about 4.0 MeV. Using the mass for the $K^\pm$ kaon given above, we find the mass of the $K^0$ or its antiparticle $\overline{K^0}$ to be

$$m_{K^0} \text{ (neutral kaon)} = 497.8 \text{ MeV}$$

### HYPERONS

The mass of the $\Lambda^0$ particle is obtained from a study of the kinematics of its principal mode of decay $\Lambda^0 \rightarrow p + \pi^-$. Measurement of the energies and momenta of the two charged decay products and of the angle between the tracks determines the incident momentum of the $\Lambda^0$ particle from which, with the masses and energies of the proton and pion products, the mass of the $\Lambda^0$ particle is found to be 1115.4 MeV. The $\Lambda^0$ particle is an example of a neutral singlet; no charged $\Lambda$ particles have been found.

The mass of the charged $\Sigma^+$ particle has been obtained from the kinematics in the decay processes $\Sigma^+ \rightarrow n + \pi^+$ and $\Sigma^+ \rightarrow p + \pi^0$ in a manner similar to that described in earlier examples and has the value 1189.2 MeV. The mass difference between $\Sigma^-$ and $\Sigma^+$ comes from kinematic analysis of the two processes $K^- + p \rightarrow \Sigma^- + \pi^+$ and $K^- + p \rightarrow \Sigma^+ + \pi^-$. From this difference the value for the mass of the $\Sigma^-$ particle is found to be 1197.6 MeV. This is the only example in Table 2 in which positive and negative members of a particle family are not particle-antiparticle pairs. The $\Sigma^+$ and $\Sigma^-$ have different mass values; each has its antiparticle of the opposite charge. The neutral $\Sigma^0$ particle can be produced through the charge-exchange reaction $\Sigma^- + p \rightarrow \Sigma^0 + n$ and decays through the reaction $\Sigma^0 \rightarrow \Lambda^0 + \gamma$. The mass difference between the negative and neutral particles obtained from the production reaction leads to a mass for the $\Sigma^0$ particle of 1193 MeV.

The production and decay reactions of the $\Xi^-$ particle ($K^- + p \rightarrow \Xi^- + K^+$ and $\Xi^- \rightarrow \Lambda^0 + \pi^-$) have been used in a similar way to determine its mass, which is 1321.0 MeV. The mass of the neutral $\Xi^0$ particle has been determined from a few kinematic analyses of the production events, $K^- + p \rightarrow \Xi^0 + K^0$, and the subsequent decays, $\Xi^0 \rightarrow \Lambda^0 + \pi^0$, to give a value of 1310 MeV.

The application of basic symmetry principles through the theoretical techniques of special unitary group theory [SU(3)] to the group of known baryons (see Chap. 12) was used by Gell-Mann to predict a charge-singlet state which he called the $\Omega^-$ particle with a mass of 1676 MeV. It was searched for experimentally and found in 1964 to be produced through the reaction $K^- + p \rightarrow \Omega^- + K^+ + K^0$ and to decay through the reaction $\Omega^- \rightarrow \Xi^- + \pi^0$. Later a few additional examples were found. When the events were kinematically analyzed, the mass of the $\Omega^-$ particle was determined to be essentially that predicted, namely, 1675 MeV. The unique feature of the $\Omega^-$ particle is that it has a strangeness number of $-3$ (see Chap. 9); the success of the theoretical prediction has heightened interest in the use of group theory in the analysis of nucleon states. This development is discussed in more detail in Chap. 12.

*chapter 7*

# PARITY: THE MIRROR WORLD

THERE ARE MANY EXAMPLES in nature, such as crystals, plants, and microorganisms, displaying symmetry of form. Nature seems to have a built-in symmetry between right and left. In many of the most elementary natural forms there is complete identity between the form and its mirror image. These phenomena can be described by the general concept of space symmetry or as examples of invariance under space inversion.

The laws of classical physics have always shown complete symmetry between the left and the right. The mirror image of any physical process depicts another process which is governed by the same physical laws as the process itself. Consider a solenoidal electric coil producing a magnetic field which is upward in the laboratory, and an electron beam crossing this field and being deflected to the left. Viewed in a mirror, the current would produce a magnetic field which is downward, and the deflection of the beam would be to the right (see Fig. 7.1). Both of these processes satisfy the basic electromagnetic equations. The space-inverted view of this experiment looks just as reasonable as the true view and obeys the same physical laws. Although some features of the mirror view might look odd, such as the reversed printed symbols in Fig. 7.1, there is nothing in the physical process itself in the mirror view which violates reality. When analyzed in this way, all classical physical processes are found to have valid mirror images.

For our present purpose, we wish to see how mirror symmetry applies in particle interactions. Let us consider the simplest situation in which a particle at rest decays into two other particles, such as a charged pion decaying into a muon and a neutrino. For simplicity, assume the muon to be ejected upward and to have its intrinsic spin vector ($s = \frac{1}{2}$) oriented downward. Con-

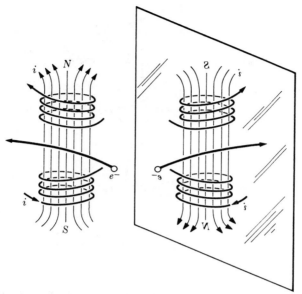

**Fig. 7.1** *Mirror view of deflection of an electron beam by a magnetic field.*

servation of momentum requires that the neutrino be ejected downward. If angular momentum is to be conserved, the neutrino spin (also $s = \frac{1}{2}$) must be oriented upward, that is, opposite the direction of the neutrino velocity vector. Now look at this process in a mirror, as illustrated in Fig. 7.2. In the mirror view the muon is still moving upward and the neutrino downward. But the directions of both spin vectors are reversed such that for both particles the spin vectors are in the same direction as the velocity vectors. This represents a process in which the relative sense of spin-to-velocity is reversed, for both particles, from that assumed to be the case in the laboratory. This process is an allowed and possible one only if both orientations of spin-to-velocity exist and are equally probable in nature. Before 1956, it was generally assumed that there was no preferred spin-to-velocity sense in nature, that either direction of *helicity* was

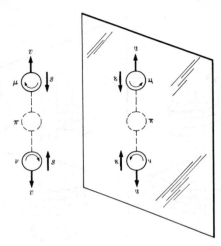

**Fig. 7.2** *Mirror view of the $\pi \rightarrow$ $\mu + \nu$ decay process.*

allowed, and that both the true and the mirror processes were valid. This agreed with the general belief that there is complete symmetry between left and right for all physical processes.

### PARITY

The parity conservation principle expresses this symmetry between events in the real world and their mirror images, this right-left symmetry of form. Parity is a mathematical term in wave mechanics which describes a classification into two groups of the wave functions representing particles, which are either even $(+)$ or odd $(-)$. A particle wave function is to a good approximation the product of one function depending on the three space coordinates and another function depending on spin orientation. When all spatial coordinates are "reflected at the origin" (signs reversed) and the sign of the spatial wave function remains unchanged, the particle has even $(+)$ parity; if the sign of the spatial wave function changes, parity is odd $(-)$. Parity is a fundamental property of the motion according to the wave-mechanical description, but it has no simple analogy in ordinary mechanics.

Parity describes whether the spatial parts of the wave functions are symmetrical or antisymmetrical. The algebraic function $y = \cos x$ is symmetrical and has the same form when reversed right-left, that is, $f(x) = +f(-x)$; its parity is even $(+)$ (see Fig. 7.3). On the other hand, the function $y = \sin x$ is

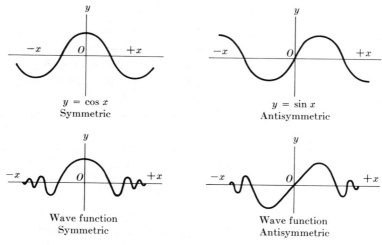

$y = \cos x$
Symmetric

$y = \sin x$
Antisymmetric

Wave function
Symmetric

Wave function
Antisymmetric

**Fig. 7.3**     *Symmetric and antisymmetric functions.*

antisymmetrical; when reversed right-left $f(x) = -f(-x)$; its parity is odd $(-)$. Wave functions which represent particles or systems of particles, which are bounded in space, are also either symmetric or antisymmetric. Purely hypothetical wave functions representing both types are also illustrated in Fig. 7.3. Such examples are not really adequate to illustrate the parity but are useful only as analogies.

The intrinsic parity of a particle can be either even $(+)$ or odd $(-)$. It is a description of a symmetry property of the spatial shape of its wave function. So long as the particle retains its identity and does not change (that is, does not decay), its parity does not change. The symbols $(+1)$ and $(-1)$ are used to identify the intrinsic parities of the particles listed in Table 2. Parity is even $(+1)$ for leptons, nucleons, and other baryons; it is odd $(-1)$ for photons and mesons. Together with the intrinsic spin, it is one of the basic properties which distinguish the different classes of particles.

This symmetry property of the mathematical expressions for wave functions was used first in atomic theory and later in nuclear theory. A compact symbolism has been developed to designate not only particles but also excitation states, in which the symbol for parity is attached as a superscript to the symbol for spin. For example, $(\frac{1}{2}^+)$ means spin $\frac{1}{2}$ and even parity; $(0^-)$ means zero spin and odd parity. This shorthand symbolism has been adopted and used in particle physics. In Chap. 10 the particle states known as resonances are identified by such symbols.

The parity of a wave function representing a system of particles includes the intrinsic parities of each of the individual particles and also depends on the relative angular momentum of the several particles. It can be shown that the contribution to the parity of the system due to the orbital angular momentum is even $(+)$ when the angular momentum quantum number is even $(l = 0, 2, \ldots)$ and odd $(-)$ when angular momentum is odd $(l = 1, 3, \ldots)$. The parity of a system of two (or more) particles is given by the algebraic product of the intrinsic parity terms and an angular momentum term, $(-1)^l$,

$$P = (P_i) \times (P_j) \times \cdots \times (-1)^l \tag{7.1}$$

where $P_i$ and $P_j$ are the intrinsic parities and $l$ is the vector sum of the angular momenta of the system. For example, in the deuterium nucleus the proton and neutron each occupy the lowest possible energy states, in which their orbital angular momenta are opposed and cancel, so $l = 0$; the parity terms are even $(+)$ for the proton, the neutron, and the angular momentum term, so the parity of the deuteron is even $(+)$. However, the intrinsic spins of the proton and neutron add vectorially to give the deuteron a spin angular momentum of unity.

The concept of symmetry of wave functions involves more than just the parity. The symmetry properties of the complete wave function, including the spin as well as the spatial coordinates, determine the "statistics" of particles (see Chap. 3). If the complete wave function is antisymmetric, the particle obeys the Fermi-Dirac statistics. The wave function including the spin coordinates can be antisymmetric, even though the spatial part may be symmetric. All leptons and nucleons obey the Fermi-Dirac statistics and have intrinsic spin $s = \frac{1}{2}$; the hyperons listed in Table 2 also have half-integral spin. However, if the complete wave function is symmetric, the particle obeys the Bose-Einstein statistics and has zero or integral spin. The class of particles called mesons in Table 2 all have 0 spin; some of the meson resonances discussed in Chap. 10 have integral spin.

## CONSERVATION OF PARITY

*Parity is conserved* in an interaction if the algebraic product of all parity terms entering the reaction is the same afterward. The parity of the initial state of the system is the product of the intrinsic parities of the particles involved and the angular momentum term [Eq. (7.1)]; the parity of the final state is the same product of the intrinsic parities of the product particles and their angular-momentum term. We noted earlier that the parity term coming from the angular momentum is even $(+)$ if $l$ is even $(l = 0, 2, \ldots)$ and odd $(-)$ if $l$ is odd $(l = 1, 3, \ldots)$.

It is believed that parity is conserved in all interactions in atomic physics, that is, all those which involve the electromagnetic interactions between the charged particles of the atom. Parity is also conserved in nuclear interactions involving the strong nuclear force. The parity of a nucleus can be changed only by the capture or emission of photons or particles which have odd total parity (intrinsic parity times parity of relative motion). For example, if an $\alpha$ particle (which has even intrinsic parity) is emitted with $l = 1$ with respect to the emitting nucleus, the total parity is odd and the parity of the product nucleus will be changed.

One aspect of parity conservation is right-left symmetry. There appears to be no distinction between right and left in the strong interactions or in the electromagnetic interactions. This means that there is no preferred helicity of emitted particles and no preference in the direction of emission relative to the orientation of the emitted particle spin vector. In strong interactions between beams of polarized protons (which all have the same vector direction of their spins in space) and polarized targets, the yields parallel and antiparallel to the direction of polarization are the same in the center-of-mass coordinate system. In radioactive decay processes in which $\gamma$ rays are emitted, involving the electromagnetic interaction, they have no preferred direction; just as many emerge downward as upward from polarized nuclei.

Conservation of parity in the strong interactions can be illustrated with the analysis used by Panofsky in 1951 to determine the intrinsic parity of the negative pion $\pi^-$. Panofsky was studying the capture of $\pi^-$ pions in deuterium, for which the dominant process is

$$\pi^- + d \rightarrow n + n \qquad\qquad (7.2)$$

The negative pion, when slowed down by collisions and ionizing impacts, is readily captured in a Bohr orbit in the deuterium atom. This orbit of the mesic atom is much smaller than an electron orbit because of the large pion mass, and the pion has a large probability of interacting with the nucleus. Theoretically, the capture interaction proceeds from the lowest energy state of the $(\pi^-, d)$ system, for which $l = 0$. Since the $\pi^-$ pion has 0 spin, the total angular momentum of the system is that of the deuteron spin alone, which is 1. The parity of this system is that of the $\pi^-$ pion alone, since the intrinsic parity of the deuteron is even and $l = 0$.

Now consider the final state of the interaction, Eq. (7.2), the state which involves two neutrons $(n,n)$. For angular momentum to be conserved, the total angular momentum including their spins must be 1. However, the Pauli exclusion principle forbids two neutrons with parallel spins to occupy the same energy state; so one of the neutrons must be in a higher energy state for which the orbital angular momentum $l = 1$. Therefore, since the parity of each neutron is even, the parity of the $(n,n)$ state is odd. But the parity of the initial $(\pi^-,d)$ system was shown above to be that of the $\pi^-$ alone. Thus, the intrinsic parity of the $\pi^-$ pion must be odd $(-)$.

The pion occurs in three charge states, $\pi^+$, $\pi^-$, and $\pi^0$, which form an *isotopic-spin* triplet, discussed in Chap. 8. The theory based on isotopic spin would be untenable if the three pions had different spins or different parities. There is also experimental evidence that the spins of the three pions are all zero and that their intrinsic parities are all odd $(-)$.

The technique of applying the test for parity conservation involves theoretical analyses which go beyond the scope of this survey. For our present purpose, we wish only to establish the concept of parity as a description of an important symmetry property of nature and to show that parity is a "good" quantum number in strong nuclear interactions and electromagnetic interactions.

Scientists, philosophers, and others have been interested in the significance of space-inversion invariance. If parity is conserved and the above conclusions are correct, nature does not distinguish between right and left, even in atomic or nuclear systems. Science fiction writers have speculated on the difficulties of communicating our definitions of right and left to intelligences in another world, if nature itself makes no distinction.

## BREAKDOWN OF PARITY CONSERVATION

In 1956 a challenge to the universality of parity conservation arose which was called the "$\theta$-$\tau$ puzzle." These heavy mesons (now known as kaons) were under intensive study during the years 1954 to 1956. They seemed to consist of two types, $\theta$ and $\tau$, which were otherwise identical but were observed to decay in different ways. The $\theta$ decayed into two pions while the $\tau$ decayed into three pions

$$K^+ \left\{ \begin{array}{l} \theta^+ \rightarrow \pi^+ + \pi^0 \\ \tau^+ \rightarrow \pi^+ + \pi^+ + \pi^- \end{array} \right. \tag{7.3}$$

The pions had been shown to have odd parity, so in the decay into two pions, the combination must be even and the parent $\theta$ meson should have even parity. In the decay into three pions a similar (but somewhat more complicated) analysis shows that the $\tau$ should have odd parity. Meanwhile, measurements of increasing accuracy showed the two mesons to have the same masses and to behave identically in other respects.

In searching for an answer to this puzzle, T. D. Lee and C. N. Yang in 1956 reexamined the basis for the generally held conviction that parity is always conserved and found no evidence for this conclusion for weak interactions, of which this decay process is an example. They proposed that parity need not be conserved in weak interactions and that the $\theta$ and $\tau$ mesons could be the same particle having two modes of decay. The kaon is now known to have odd parity; so it is the two-pion decay mode (the most probable) in which parity conservation is violated.

Lee and Yang further noted that if parity is not conserved in other weak interactions, it could lead to an asymmetry in the direction of emission of $\beta$ rays from spin-polarized radioactive nuclei. In an experimental test by C. S. Wu, aided by a group from the National Bureau of Standards, radioactive cobalt atoms were used whose nuclei were polarized in a magnetic field and which decayed with the emission of $\beta$ ray electrons and antineutrinos

$$_{27}\text{Co}^{60} \rightarrow {}_{28}\text{Ni}^{60} + e^- + \overline{\nu}_e \qquad (7.4)$$

The experiment was performed at liquid-helium temperatures to avoid thermal disturbance of the polarization. The intensity of electrons emitted parallel and antiparallel to the direction of magnetic field, which determines the direction of polarization of the $\text{Co}^{60}$ nuclei, was measured. These measurements did not require any change in the physical geometry of the experiment but involved only reversal of the magnetic field. The results showed an asymmetry with more electrons emitted antiparallel to the field than parallel to the field. All other parts of the apparatus, such as the coils and currents producing the fields, have left-right symmetry; so the observed asymmetry must be attributed to the disintegration of the Co nuclei, which is a weak interaction. More electrons were emitted opposite the direction of the $\text{Co}^{60}$ polarization than in this direction.

This experiment also demonstrates a correlation between the direction of the emitted particle and the orientation of its own spin vector, both for the electrons and for the antineutrinos. More electrons are emitted preferentially opposite the direction of electron spin than parallel to the spin; thus the electron is "left handed" in the sense that its spin rotation is that of a left-handed screw. The orientation of the antineutrino requires a more detailed analysis and is discussed in the following section. That asymmetry was observed is sufficient to prove that parity conservation is violated in this weak interaction. If parity were conserved this asymmetry would not exist and the electrons would be emitted symmetrically and independent of the direction of polarization of the $\text{Co}^{60}$ nucleus.

This result suggested that similar asymmetries might be observed in other weak interactions. Pion beams were available at several accelerator laboratories, where experiments were arranged to study the decay of pions into muons and $\mu$ neutrinos. The first definitive experiment was performed by R. Garwin, L. Lederman et al. from Columbia University, using $\pi^+$ pion beams from the Nevis cyclotron. The decay process is

$$\pi^+ \rightarrow \mu^+ + \nu_\mu \qquad (T = 1.8 \times 10^{-8} \text{ sec}) \qquad (7.5)$$

followed by

$$\mu^+ \rightarrow e^+ + \nu_e + \nu_\mu \qquad (T = 1.5 \times 10^{-6} \text{ sec}) \qquad (7.6)$$

The pions were brought to low energies by absorbers in the beam; they then decayed into muons. Some of the pions decayed in flight, and their muon products were projected forward where they entered and came to rest within a block of carbon in which they decayed. A magnetic field superposed on the carbon absorber caused precession of the spins of the positive muons at a rate calculable from their known magnetic moments. When they decayed, the final positron product was observed in counters placed at different azimuthal locations around the beam axis, so that the magnitude of the precession (and its right-left sense) could be observed. Time-delay circuits were arranged to observe each $\pi^+ \rightarrow \mu^+$, $\mu^+ \rightarrow e^+$ sequence electronically and to observe the amount of precession. From these observations the conclusion was drawn that the spin of the muon is directed preferentially opposite its direction of emission in the pion decay process [Eq. (7.5)]. In other words, positive muons are found to be left-handed when emitted from the pion. This is another example of violation of parity conservation in another weak interaction.

From these experimental results it is possible to draw the general conclusion that parity need not be conserved for any of the weak interactions, which agrees with the prediction of Lee and Yang. We are justified in applying further theoretical considerations consistent with this prediction. For example, many properties are reversed between particles and antiparticles. If there is a constraint on nature restricting its freedom to be completely symmetrical, we might expect such a basic property as a preferred spin orientation (the helicity) to be reversed for antiparticles. The present concept is that if a particle has one helicity, its antiparticle of the same class will have the opposite helicity. If $\beta$-ray electrons are left-handed, radioactively emitted positrons should be right-handed. The same reversal should apply between neutrinos and antineutrinos. In the following section we will see that the facts confirm these generalizations.

Some interesting physical and philosophical consequences follow from this result. We see that nature does have a built-in sense of right or left. There is a preferred direction of the spin of a newly created particle coming from a weak interaction, which differs for the different particles. This does not mean that the spins of all electrons in motion, for example, are always aligned opposite their direction of motion, but only that there is a preferred alignment when they are created and emitted from nuclei as $\beta$ rays. In fact, we know that electron spins can be "flipped" from one orientation to another in an atom, while the electron maintains its state of motion, by application of radio-frequency fields of the exact energy to resonate with the change in energy state of the electron in the atom (see Chap. 5). A beam of electrons can be polarized either parallel, antiparallel, or transverse to its direction of motion, and the orientation of polarization can be changed at will by application of suitable magnetic and radiofrequency fields.

Another conclusion now possible has been appropriated by writers of science fiction. It should be possible to communicate our definition of right or left to intelligences in another world by transmitting a complete description of an experiment on the asymmetry of $\beta$-ray emission from aligned nuclei. From their response we could then determine whether their world was formed of matter or antimatter.

### SPIN CORRELATIONS IN WEAK INTERACTIONS

From the experimental results on asymmetry in weak-interaction decay, and from general conservation principles, it is possible to identify the helicities—the specific correlations between spin and direction—for each of the products in weak-interaction decays. This requires caution, however, since helicity must be defined relative to a particular coordinate system. For example, if an electron is emitted from a beta decay process with velocity $v = 0.95c$ and is observed in the laboratory to have left-handed helicity, its helicity would be reversed if viewed from a coordinate system moving parallel to the particle with velocity $v = 0.99c$. So any particle with a finite rest mass can only have its helicity defined relative to a particular coordinate system. However, zero-mass particles such as neutrinos will not have their helicities changed by change of coordinate system, since they move with the velocity of light. Helicity is a firm property of zero-mass particles and remains the same as in the emission process.

The beta decay process is complicated by the parent and product nuclei, which participate in the momentum recoil and in spin conservation. The parent and product nuclei in a beta decay process have either the same total angular momentum ($\Delta l = 0$), or they differ by an integral value of angular momentum ($\Delta l = 1$). In the first case (Fermi transitions) where $\Delta l = 0$, the half-integral spins of the electron and antineutrino must be opposed in direction and cancel for spin to be conserved in the transition. In the second type (Gamow-Teller transitions) where $\Delta l = 1$, the only way in which spin can be conserved is for the spins of the electron and the antineutrino to be parallel and to add vectorially to one.

The transition which occurs in the $Co^{60}$ decay [Eq. (7.4)] is of the Gamow-Teller type. $_{27}Co^{60}$ is an "odd-$Z$, odd-$N$" nucleus for which the total angular momentum is known to be 1, while $_{28}Ni^{60}$ is an "even-$Z$, even-$N$" nucleus for which the angular momentum is 0. So the half-integral spins of the electron and antineutrino must be parallel for their sum to cancel the $\Delta l = 1$ of the nuclei. Kinematic analysis of this relativistic decay process shows that there is also a strong correlation in direction of emission of the two products; the electron and the antineutrino are emitted in opposite directions (in the relativistic limit). The experiments by Wu et al. show that the electron is emitted preferentially opposite the direction of its spin (left-handed). For the two spins to add, the antineutrino spin must be parallel to its direction, that is, the antineutrino must be right-handed.

For completeness, the process in a Fermi transition should be described. With $\Delta l = 0$ for the parent and product nuclei, the spins of the electron and the antineutrino must be opposed and cancel. This can occur only if the directions of emission of the two are parallel—they must go off together. With this restriction imposed by conservation of spin, the only way in which momentum can be conserved is for the product nucleus to participate and to recoil with a momentum equal and opposite to the sum of the momenta of the two light products.

Consider next the radioactive decay of neutron-deficient nuclei which yield positrons, such as

$$_{15}P^{30} \rightarrow {}_{14}Si^{30} + \overline{e^+} + \nu_e \tag{7.7}$$

The positron is the antiparticle of the electron and is accompanied in the decay by an electron neutrino (a particle). We assume that the spin-direction orientation of the $e^+$ is opposite that for the $e^-$, that is, that it is right-handed. The decay process is of the Gamow-Teller type, as for $Co^{60}$, and $\Delta l = 1$. The same conclusions can be drawn that the positron and the electron neutrino are emitted in opposite directions, with their spins adding. So the electron neutrino has a spin opposite its direction, that is, it is left-handed.

In both types of $\beta$-ray transition the degree of longitudinal polarization of the emitted electrons (or positrons) depends on the velocity of emission through the relativistic parameter $v/c$. For electrons with very high velocities the asymmetry is large with a high degree of spin polarization in the direction of emission; for slower electrons the degree of asymmetry is not so great. As a consequence, the physical description given above is only a crude approximation, which is given in detail by a theoretical analysis of the process.

Now consider the processes of pion decay into muons. Here the analysis is simpler, since it is a free particle decaying into two product particles and no nucleus is involved. In the last section, the $\pi^+$ decay [Eq. (7.5)] was shown to result in a $\overline{\mu^+}$ (antiparticle) with a spin opposite its direction, that is, left-handed, and a muon neutrino. Conservation of momentum requires that the two particles be emitted in opposite directions. Conservation of spin requires the spin of the muon neutrino to cancel that of the muon; so the muon neutrino is also left-handed.

Negative pions can also decay into muons and anti-muon-neutrinos in the absence of matter in which they might otherwise form mesic atoms. The process is

$$\pi^- \longrightarrow \mu^- + \overline{\nu_\mu} \tag{7.8}$$

In this case, the spins of the muons are preferentially aligned parallel to the direction of emission, and so are right-handed. For spin to be conserved, the $\overline{\nu_\mu}$ must also be right-handed.

In Fig. 7.4 these conclusions about the initial orientations of spin and direction of emission are summarized for all eight of the leptons involved in weak interactions. Some interesting correlations can be noted. Both the electron neutrino and the $\mu$ neutrino are left-handed and are identical in this respect as well as in their other properties. The two antineutrinos are both right-handed. The preferred helicity of the $\mu^-$muon in $\pi$ decay is right-handed, opposite that of the electron in beta decay. The significance of helicity for particles with rest mass is questionable, as discussed above, and seems to have no bearing on the basic problem why the muon exists.

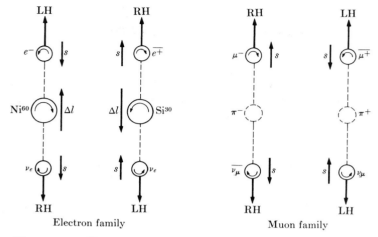

**Fig. 7.4**   *Helicity orientations for leptons in weak interaction decays.*

Charged pions decay primarily through the muon mode, as illustrated in Eq. (7.5). They also decay with the emission of electrons through the much rarer mode

$$\pi^\pm \rightarrow e^\pm + \left\{ \begin{array}{c} \nu_e \\ \bar{\nu}_e \end{array} \right. \tag{7.9}$$

In this case the helicities also conserve angular momentum, if the electron and its antineutrino are both left-handed, agreeing with the conclusions above. The suppression of the electron mode depends on a theoretical argument involving the mass of the particle; if the rest mass of the electron were zero this reaction would not occur.

A similar correlation between spin and direction is observed in other decay processes involving the weak interaction. For example, consider the production and decay of the $\Lambda^0$

$$\pi^- + p \rightarrow \Lambda^0 + K^0 \tag{7.10}$$

$$\Lambda^0 \rightarrow p + \pi^- \tag{7.11}$$

The production process is a fast reaction involving the strong nuclear force, in which the trajectories of the $\pi^-$, $\Lambda^0$, and $K^0$ establish a plane. The orientation of this plane in space is determined by the spin direction of the particular target proton, and the spin of the $\Lambda^0$ is also oriented relative to this plane. The most probable spin orientations for the $p$ and $\Lambda^0$ are perpendicular to the plane to conserve angular momentum. (Note that the $\pi^-$ and $K^0$ both have zero spin and are not oriented.) This spin orientation of the $\Lambda^0$ is observed in the decay process [Eq (7.11)] which is a weak interaction, where the protons are found to be emitted preferentially on one side of the plane defined above and the pions on the other side. As another example of nonconservation of parity in a weak interaction, it shows a correlation between spin and direction for the product proton, a correlation which is not observed in strong interactions. Apparently, the distinction between right and left in nature is not restricted to leptons but also occurs with baryons when they are produced and emitted in weak interactions.

We can conclude that the violation of parity conservation in the weak interactions is as important a fact of nature as its conservation in the strong and electromagnetic interactions.

*chapter 8*

# CHARGE
# INDEPENDENCE
# AND
# ISOTOPIC SPIN

THE FORCES THAT BIND NUCLEAR PARTICLES together are evidence for the strong nuclear interaction. These strong forces are also involved in the interactions between protons, neutrons, and mesons which occur at very high energies and in very short times. These interactions include the scattering of one particle by another, the production of new particles, including mesons or heavier products, the annihilation of antiparticles, etc. In most of the interactions of interest the incident particles have very high energy and velocities close to that of light. The time to cross a nucleon and interact is extremely short (of the order of $10^{-23}$ sec). We call these interactions strong because even in this brief time the force is strong enough to cause the interaction.

Nature applies certain constraints on these strong interactions, certain limitations which allow some interactions to occur and others not to occur. Our method of systematizing experimental evidence is to formulate conservation principles and selection rules which apply. In this case, two new conservation laws, isotopic spin and strangeness, which are discussed in this and the following chapter, have been introduced to describe the special properties of the strong interactions. The isotopic-spin conservation law is limited in its application to the strong interactions and is in addition to the five classical conservation laws described in Chap. 5 and the parity conservation principle discussed in Chap. 7.

## CHARGE INDEPENDENCE

When the neutron was identified as a component of nuclei, with a mass very nearly that of the proton but with zero charge, it became necessary to consider the problem of nuclear stability.

Protons and neutrons must attract each other with a very strong nuclear force of a completely new type. The two particles are found to have many similarities, particularly with respect to the energy levels which they occupy in nuclei. For example, in the "mirror" nuclei among the light elements ($H^3$–$He^3$, $Li^7$–$Be^7$, $Be^9$–$B^9$, $C^{13}$–$N^{13}$, etc.), in which the number of nucleons is the same but the numbers of protons and neutrons are interchanged, the binding energies and the excited states are almost the same in each pair, and the small differences can be explained by the electromagnetic effects of the different nuclear charges. Furthermore, studies of proton-proton and proton-neutron scattering show that the purely nuclear interactions are identical. The nuclear force between the two particles is independent of whether they are charged or neutral. From such evidence, the proton and neutron came to be recognized at an early stage as two substates of the same basic particle state, which we call the nucleon.

### ISOTOPIC SPIN

This charge independence of nuclear forces led Heisenberg to propose the concept of "charge" space and a quantum number called *isotopic spin* to identify the two charge substates in which the nucleon exists. Isotopic spin can be represented by a vector with quantized components having unique directions, analogous to the vectors used earlier in quantum mechanics to describe spin and angular momentum in atomic and nuclear physics. In isotopic-spin space ($I$ space), the nucleon is a doublet with two charge states, positive and neutral. This parallels the spin doublet $(+\frac{1}{2}, -\frac{1}{2})$ of the electron which has half-integral spin and which is represented by a vector having two directions, parallel and antiparallel to the direction of the orbital angular momentum vector.

To utilize the theoretical relationships and the quantum-mechanical bookkeeping developed for the spin quantum number, the terminology and the assignment of quantum numbers for isotopic spin have been taken (somewhat arbitrarily) directly from past practice in describing spin. Since the exchange of one nucleon for another in nuclei leads to isotopes (actually, isobars), this new kind of spin is called isotopic spin. The name is a misnomer based on this analogy; it has nothing whatsoever to do with isotopes as the term is used in nuclear physics, nor with any mechanical or quantum concept of spin or angular momentum.

Heisenberg's concept of isotopic spin was the basis for a mathematical description of atomic phenomena useful in nuclear physics. However, it was many years before the full significance and physical content of the concept became evident with the discovery of the several families of strange particles in the 1950s; these particles had similar masses and other properties but occurred in different charge states. A number of charge multiplets were observed among the strange particles, including singlets, doublets, and triplets. This experimental evidence greatly enhanced the significance and usefulness of the concept of isotopic spin.

Singlet isotopic spin states are assigned the quantum number $I = 0$; examples are the $\Lambda^0$ and $\Omega^-$ particles, each of which has only one charge state. Doublet states are assigned isotopic spin $I = \frac{1}{2}$ and include particles which have two charge states such as the nucleon (positive and zero) and the $\Xi$ particle (zero and negative). Triplets are assigned isotopic spin $I = 1$ and include those particles which have positive, neutral, and negative members, such as the pion and the $\Sigma$ particle.

When the extremely short-lived states called resonances were observed and studied (see Chap. 10), the value of the isotopic spin concept became even more evident. The $N_1^*$ resonance was found to have isotopic spin $I = \frac{3}{2}$. According to quantum-mechanical principles, the number of substates or the multiplicity $M$ of an angular-momentum vector $l$ is given by $M = 2l + 1$. For $l = \frac{3}{2}$, there will be four substates, which can be visualized as having the four vector orientations $\frac{3}{2}$, $\frac{1}{2}$, $-\frac{1}{2}$, $-\frac{3}{2}$. Charge occurs only in integral multiples of the electronic charge $q$.   The interpretation of the four charge substates indicated by an isotopic spin of $\frac{3}{2}$ is that the four members have charges of $2q$, $1q$, 0, and $-1q$, respectively.   Here is the first example in nature of a particle state which has more than a single unit of electric charge. Unfortunately, it is not possible to observe the doubly charged state of the $N_1^*$ resonance directly because of its extremely short lifetime.   Evidence for its existence comes from the assumption of conservation of charge in the production process and in the observation of other properties consistent with a state having isotopic spin $\frac{3}{2}$.

## THIRD COMPONENT OF ISOTOPIC SPIN

Isotopic spin $I$ is a vector in charge space whose magnitude determines the number of allowed orientations of this vector, given by the multiplicity $M = 2I + 1$.   Each of the allowed orientations defines a particular charge substate.   The *third component* of isotopic spin $I_3$ is the component or charge substate which is parallel to the isotopic spin axis for the particular sub-state.   This symbolism parallels the use of the *z component* of angular momentum in the formalism of quantum mechanics, where the $z$ component is parallel to the total angular momentum axis.

The third component can be specified for each member of a charge multiplet.   For singlet states with $I = 0$, the third component $I_3 = 0$.   For doublet states with $I = \frac{1}{2}$, the third component $I_3 = +\frac{1}{2}$ for the "most positive" member and $I = -\frac{1}{2}$ for the "most negative" member; for example, $I_3 = +\frac{1}{2}$ for the proton and $-\frac{1}{2}$ for the neutron in the nucleon doublet; and $I_3 = +\frac{1}{2}$ for the neutral and $-\frac{1}{2}$ for the negative member of the $\Xi$ doublet.   For triplet states with $I = 1$, which have positive, neutral, and negative charge substates, the values of $I_3$ are $+1$, 0, and $-1$, respectively.   In the special case of a quadruplet state, such as the $N_1^*$ resonance described above for which

$I = \frac{3}{2}$, the values of $I_3$ are $+\frac{3}{2}$, $+\frac{1}{2}$, $-\frac{1}{2}$, and $-\frac{3}{2}$ for the four substates with charges of $2q$, $1q$, $0$, and $1 - q$, respectively. Values for the third component $I_3$ for each of the observable particles involved in strong interactions are listed in Table 2. For antiparticles, the signs of the third components are reversed in recognition of the reversal of charge for antiparticles.

### CONSERVATION OF ISOTOPIC SPIN

The quantum number $I$, used to specify the isotopic spin of a charge multiplet, is an intrinsically positive number which defines the number of charge substates in the multiplet. The isotopic spin is the same for antiparticles as for particles, since the number of charge states in antispace is the same as in real space.

*Conservation of isotopic spin* means that there is no change in the vector sum of isotopic spins during an interaction. The probability of any process, or the strength of the interaction, is unchanged if the isotopic spin vector is "rotated" in $I$ space in a manner in which the total isotopic spin (number of charge states) is conserved.

Isotopic spin is conserved in all strong nuclear interactions. In those interactions which involve the strong nuclear force, nature does not care whether a particle carries an electric charge or not, but only whether the total number of charge states remains constant. Protons and neutrons act identically as far as their purely nuclear interactions are concerned. Positive, negative, and neutral pions all interact with nucleons, or are produced, with the same probability. Interactions between nucleons and pions in which the signs of the charges are interchanged but which represent only a "rotation" of the charge vector in $I$ space have the same cross section. An example is in the two scattering processes $(\pi^+,p)$ and $(\pi^-,n)$, which occur with equal probabilities.

The third component of isotopic spin is also conserved for all strong nuclear interactions. Third component $I_3$ defines the orientation of the charge vector in $I$ space for each component of a charge multiplet. Since $I_3$ is defined relative to the same vector axis for all particles involved in an interaction, the algebraic sum of third components is the quantity conserved. Let us illustrate conservation of isotopic spin and its third component with the strong interactions between charged pions and protons. First, with positive pions, the only two-product interaction allowed by charge conservation is elastic scattering

$$\pi^+ + p \rightarrow \pi^+ + p \qquad (8.1)$$

Isotopic spin is a vector. For pions $I = 1$ and for nucleons $I = \frac{1}{2}$, the vector sum could be $\frac{3}{2}$ or $\frac{1}{2}$ and must be conserved. To find which value of $I$ is involved, consider the third components. $I_3 = +1$ for $\pi^+$ and $I_3 = +\frac{1}{2}$ for the proton; the algebraic sum of $I_3$ components is $+\frac{3}{2}$, and therefore the total isotopic spin $I$ must be $\frac{3}{2}$.

However, with negative pions two interactions are allowed by charge conservation, elastic scattering, and charge exchange

$$\pi^- + p \rightarrow \pi^- + p \qquad (8.2)$$
$$\text{and } \pi^- + p \rightarrow \pi^0 + n \qquad (8.3)$$

Here also the vector sum of isotopic spins may be $\frac{3}{2}$ or $\frac{1}{2}$ and must be conserved. The algebraic sum of third components of the particles entering the interaction is $I_3 = -1 + \frac{1}{2} = -\frac{1}{2}$. The third component is conserved in both interactions above but through different channels: $I_3 = -1 + \frac{1}{2} = -\frac{1}{2}$ for the scattering process and $I_3 = 0 - \frac{1}{2} = -\frac{1}{2}$ for the charge-exchange reaction. Both the $I = \frac{3}{2}$ and $I = \frac{1}{2}$ states could give this result for $I_3$; so both states can exist in the $(\pi^-, p)$ system.

The experimental observations of the total scattering cross section of pions on protons as a function of pion energy are shown in Fig. 8.1. With $\pi^+$ pions, a single strong scattering peak is observed at a kinetic energy of about 180 MeV. This is associated with scattering from the isotopic-spin state of $I = \frac{3}{2}$

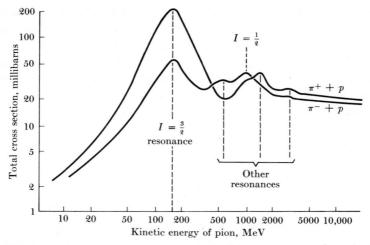

**Fig. 8.1**    *Scattering of $\pi^+$ and $\pi^-$ pions from protons as a function of pion energy.*

and is called the $\frac{3}{2}$ resonance. With $\pi^-$ pions, both isotopic-spin states are involved, so the $\frac{3}{2}$ resonance is not as prominent; part of the time the reaction proceeds through the $I = \frac{1}{2}$ channel, which occurs at about 1000 MeV for $\pi^-$ pions. The additional structure in the excitation curves at higher energies is due to other resonances, which will be discussed further in Chap. 10.

### NONCONSERVATION OF ISOTOPIC SPIN

When isotopic spin is not conserved in interactions between nuclear particles, the strong interaction is forbidden. If the strong interaction is forbidden, the process can occur only through a weaker interaction, which is generally much slower. It is just because isotopic-spin conservation is violated for all modes of decay which are allowed through other conservation laws, for all of the strange particles, that these particles cannot decay promptly but survive to decay through the much longer-lived processes of the electromagnetic or weak interactions. In fact, this property gave the strange particles their name.

Conservation of isotopic spin is violated for electromagnetic interactions. As far as we know, this is the only conservation law which is not common to the strong and the electromagnetic interactions. If isotopic spin were conserved in interactions involving the proton and neutron, charge symmetry would be complete between these two particles. With complete charge symmetry they should have the same mass. It is just because charge symmetry is violated in the electromagnetic interaction that there is a mass difference (of about 1.3 MeV) between the neutron and proton.

Electromagnetic interactions can occur, even involving particles with zero charge, where a photon is either an incident radiation or a product radiation. For example, the $\pi^0$ pion decays through the electromagnetic interaction

$$\pi^0 \to \gamma + \gamma \qquad (T = 0.7 \times 10^{-16} \text{ sec}) \qquad (8.4)$$

The isotopic spin of pions is 1, and the third component of the $\pi^0$ is 0. It is not possible to assign an isotopic-spin value other than 0 to the photon, and even this assignment has no meaning since it is not conserved. So isotopic spin is not conserved, and no value is listed for the photon.

Another electromagnetic decay process is that of the $\Sigma^0$

$$\Sigma^0 \to \Lambda^0 + \gamma \qquad (T < 10^{-14} \text{ sec}) \qquad (8.5)$$

The isotopic spin of the $\Sigma^0$ is 1 (three charge states), while that of the $\Lambda^0$ is 0 (single charge state); so conservation of isotopic spin is violated. However, it is interesting to note that third component $I_3$ is conserved in this process (if $I_3$ is taken to be 0 for the photon). It seems to be generally true that $I_3$ is conserved in electromagnetic interactions, even though $I$ is violated.

Isotopic-spin conservation is also violated in all weak interactions. This is true even though all particles involved in the weak interaction are strongly interacting particles.   As an example, consider the decay of the $\Lambda^0$

$$\Lambda^0 \rightarrow \pi^- + p$$
and $\Lambda^0 \rightarrow \pi^0 + n$    $(T = 1.8 \times 10^{-10} \text{ sec})$    (8.6)

In both of these decay processes $I$ changes from 0 to $\frac{1}{2}$ (or $\frac{3}{2}$), and third component $I_3$ changes from 0 to $-\frac{1}{2}$.   So both isotopic-spin and third-component conservations are violated.

Leptons, which include electrons, muons, and neutrinos, are never involved in strong nuclear interactions.   Their production and decay processes all proceed through the weak or electromagnetic interactions.   Isotopic spin is not involved in any of these processes; so no assignments of this quantum number are made for leptons.

*chapter 9*

# STRANGENESS

WHEN THE SEVERAL NEW TYPES of strange particles (the kaons and hyperons listed in Table 2) were being intensively studied with the first multi-billion-volt accelerators in the early 1950s, it became evident that the existing conservation principles were not adequate. The very existence of these new particles could not be understood unless some hitherto unknown property of nature was involved. It seemed that there must be some further constraint upon nature, some new symmetry principle, some new conservation law.

In 1947 G. D. Rochester and C. C. Butler of the University of Manchester reported the first evidence for the strange particles with the observation of V tracks in cloud chambers exposed to cosmic rays at high altitudes (see Fig. 4.6). But this evidence was too scanty to draw any conclusions about the properties of these particles, except for their probable existence as entities and the fact that some had masses greater than the nucleon mass. The first opportunity to study these particles in detail came when the 3-GeV cosmotron at the Brookhaven Laboratory was brought into operation in 1952 and when a large liquid-hydrogen bubble chamber with a magnetic field was installed to detect and observe the interactions in 1953.

These particles were called strange because of their unusual behavior. They were produced in high-energy collisions of strongly interacting particles such as pions and nucleons, with a high probability (large cross section) compatible with the strong nuclear interaction. The time associated with such a strong interaction is equivalent to that for a particle moving at the velocity of light to traverse a nucleon, which is of the order $10^{-23}$ sec. Yet the strange particles were observed to have very much longer lifetimes, decaying into lighter-mass products with half-lives of $10^{-8}$ to $10^{-11}$ sec. This indicated that they were not decaying through the strong interaction but through a much weaker interaction with a force constant about $10^{-13}$ of that of the strong interaction. Although their lifetimes for decay are short in the laboratory time scale, they are extremely long in the time scale of nuclear interactions.

### ASSOCIATED PRODUCTION

An early theoretical hypothesis, proposed by A. Pais, was that the strange particles are produced in pairs in strong interaction processes but, following their separation, they decay individually through a weaker interaction. This *associated production* was observed at Brookhaven in 1954 in bubble-chamber photographs of the tracks of the charged particle products of interactions between high-energy incident pions and protons in the liquid hydrogen. One of the earliest examples was the observation of two inverted V tracks produced in a single event which was initiated by an incoming 1.5-GeV negative pion, illustrated in Fig. 9.1. One of the V tracks was found to consist of a proton

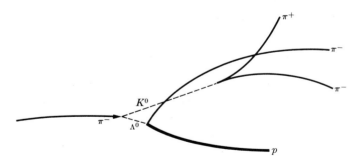

**Fig. 9.1** *Production of strange particles by pions: the "Brookhaven Interaction."*

and a negative pion; the other was a positive and negative pion pair. The apexes of both V tracks pointed toward the termination of an incoming high-energy pion track which stopped in the chamber. Presumably, the initiating event produced two neutral particles, which then decayed into the two pairs of charged particles. In the present terminology these are called the lambda-zero and the $K$-zero particles

$$\pi^- + p \to \Lambda^0 + K^0 \qquad (9.1)$$

The decay processes of these neutral particles which produce the observed V tracks are

$$\Lambda_0 \to p + \pi^- \qquad (T = 1.8 \times 10^{-10} \text{ sec}) \qquad (9.2)$$

$$K^0 \to \pi^+ + \pi^- \qquad (T = 0.7 \times 10^{-10} \text{ sec}) \qquad (9.3)$$

The distances traversed by the neutral particles before decaying are compatible with the present values of half-life for these particles (given above). The curvatures of the four charged particle tracks in the magnetic field of the bubble chamber gave a measure of their momenta, and the ionization densities allowed the particles to be identified so that their energies could be determined. By using the accepted values of rest mass for the product particles, and their energies, the mass of the neutral particles could be calculated.

### CONSERVATION OF STRANGENESS

The associated production of the strange particles and their individual stability against fast decay were the features which earned them the title "strange." To "explain" these phenomena, M. Gell-Mann and independently K. Nishijima proposed that there must be another conservation law in effect, which holds for strong interactions and permits the large production cross sections observed, but which is violated for all possible decay processes of the individual product particles. With no strong interaction decays allowed, the products will survive to decay through the weak interaction. This new conserved quality was called *strangeness.* It is described by a quantum number $S$ which is conserved (algebraic sum unchanged) in a strong interaction.

The initial assignment of strangeness numbers was somewhat arbitrary. "Normal" strongly interacting particles such as pions and nucleons were assigned $S = 0$; the $K^0$ particle was assigned $S = +1$, and the $\Lambda^0$ particle $S = -1$. But as more strange particles were found and fitted into the scheme, this assignment was found to be consistent with other related properties such as isotopic spin and baryon number assignments. It was soon discovered that strange particles occur in charge multiplets with closely similar masses, such as the $(K^+, K^0)$ doublet or the $(\Sigma^+, \Sigma^0, \Sigma^-)$ triplet. All members of such a multiplet have the same strangeness number. Antiparticles are assigned strangeness numbers opposite in sign to those for their particles.

As the experimental evidence for more and more strange particles accumulated, they were assigned strangeness numbers on the assumption that strangeness is conserved in the production processes and in other fast interactions of strange particles. Some examples of interactions leading to strangeness assignments are

$$\pi^- + p \rightarrow K^0 + \Lambda^0 \qquad \begin{cases} S = +1 \text{ for } K^0 \\ S = -1 \text{ for } \Lambda^0 \end{cases} \qquad (9.4a)$$

$$\pi^+ + n \rightarrow K^+ + \Lambda^0 \qquad S = +1 \text{ for } K^+ \qquad (9.4b)$$

$$\pi^- + p \rightarrow K^0 + \overline{K^-} + p \qquad S = -1 \text{ for } \overline{K^-} \qquad (9.4c)$$

$$\pi^+ + p \rightarrow \overline{K^0} + K^+ + p \qquad S = -1 \text{ for } \overline{K^0} \qquad (9.4d)$$

$$\pi^- + p \rightarrow K^+ + \Sigma^- \qquad S = -1 \text{ for } \Sigma^- \qquad (9.4e)$$

$$\pi^+ + n \rightarrow K^0 + \Sigma^+ \qquad S = -1 \text{ for } \Sigma^+ \qquad (9.4f)$$

$$\Sigma^- + p \rightarrow n + \Sigma^0 \qquad S = -1 \text{ for } \Sigma^0 \qquad (9.4g)$$

$$\overline{K^-} + p \rightarrow K^0 + \Xi^0 \qquad S = -2 \text{ for } \Xi^0 \qquad (9.4h)$$

$$\pi^- + p \rightarrow K^0 + K^+ + \Xi^- \qquad S = -2 \text{ for } \Xi^- \qquad (9.4i)$$

$$\overline{K^-} + p \rightarrow K^0 + K^+ + \Omega^- \qquad S = -3 \text{ for } \Omega^- \qquad (9.4j)$$

These assignments of strangeness number are listed in Table 2. Strangeness is also conserved in electromagnetic interactions if the photon is assigned $S = 0$. In one case where a photon is a product of a strange particle decay, strangeness is conserved:

$$\Sigma^0 \rightarrow \Lambda^0 + \gamma \qquad (T < 10^{-14} \text{ sec}) \qquad (9.5)$$

Strangeness conservation is violated in the slow decay of strange particles into lower mass particles and in other weak interactions involving leptons ($e^{\pm}$, $\mu^{\pm}$, and $\nu_{e,\mu}$). No strangeness numbers are assigned to leptons.

The requirement for conservation of strangeness and isotopic spin in strong interactions is the apparent reason why other possible production reactions, which might otherwise be allowed, do not occur, such as $\pi^- + p \nrightarrow \Lambda^0 + \pi^0$. Isotopic spin and strangeness conservation are both violated in this interaction; it has not been observed.

The conservation of strangeness has a close relationship to several other conservation principles, such as those for electric charge, isotopic spin, and baryon number. The charge must be integral $(+1, 0, -1)$, measured in units of electronic charge $q$. Isotopic spin $I$ describes the number of charge states of a charge multiplet, and the third component $I_3$ specifies the charge state of each component of the multiplet. Baryon number is 0 for mesons and is $\pm 1$ for baryons and antibaryons. For the several families of strongly interacting particles (hadrons) we find the following relationships:

| FAMILY | STRANGE-NESS $S$ | ISOTOPIC SPIN $I_3$ | BARYON NUMBER $A$ | CHARGE $q$ |
|---|---|---|---|---|
| $\pi^+$, $\pi^0$, $\pi^-$ | 0 | 1, 0, $-1$ | 0 | $I_3$ |
| $K^+$, $K^0$ | 1 | $\frac{1}{2}$, $-\frac{1}{2}$ | 0 | $I_3 + \frac{1}{2}$ |
| $\overline{K^0}$, $K^-$ | $-1$ | $\frac{1}{2}$, $-\frac{1}{2}$ | 0 | $I_3 - \frac{1}{2}$ |
| $p$, $n$ | 0 | $\frac{1}{2}$, $-\frac{1}{2}$ | 1 | $I_3 + \frac{1}{2}$ |
| $\Lambda^0$ | $-1$ | 0 | 1 | $I_3$ |
| $\Sigma^+$, $\Sigma_0$, $\Sigma^-$ | $-1$ | 1, 0, $-1$ | 1 | $I_3$ |
| $\Xi^0$, $\Xi^-$ | $-2$ | $\frac{1}{2}$, $-\frac{1}{2}$ | 1 | $I_3 - \frac{1}{2}$ |
| $\Omega^-$ | $-3$ | 0 | 1 | $I_3 - 1$ |

The relationships above can all be summarized in the general relation between the four quantum numbers

$$q = I_3 + \tfrac{1}{2}(S + A) \qquad (9.6)$$

Since these four quantum numbers are interrelated, only three are necessary to define a strong interaction process completely. In other words, strangeness is not a necessary new quantum number but can be represented by a combination of the other three, or any three of the four can be selected to describe a strong interaction. The three which are most commonly used are strangeness, isotopic spin (or its third component), and baryon number. In applying conservation laws to strong interactions, we use the quantum numbers $S$, $I$, and $A$. The charge $q$ enters only in checking for the conservation of total electric charge in an interaction.

## PROPERTIES OF KAONS

The heavy mesons called kaons are always produced in association with another strange particle. The $K^0$ produced with the $\Lambda^0$ in the early Brookhaven experiments was assigned strangeness $S = +1$ [see Eq. (9.4a)]. When $\pi^+$ pions were used to bombard neutrons (using heavier nuclei as targets), $K^+$ kaons were produced in association with $\Lambda^0$ particles and were also assigned $S = +1$ [(Eq. (9.4b)]. Antikaons were produced in association with kaons, such as the $\overline{K^-}$ and the $\overline{K^0}$ [Eqs. (9.4c) and (9.4d)], and were assigned $S = -1$. At higher energies the antikaons are produced with antihyperons, which have positive strangeness. The kaons themselves can interact with nucleons to produce still other strange particles. Depending on the energy available, either the $K^0$ or its antiparticle the $\overline{K^0}$ can be produced as long as strangeness is conserved with the other products.

    An example of a multistep production and decay process initiated by a $\overline{K^-}$ kaon in a liquid-hydrogen bubble chamber is illustrated in Fig. 9.2. The initial fast interaction results in three products

$$\overline{K^-} + p \rightarrow \Xi^- + \overline{K^0} + \pi^+ \tag{9.7}$$

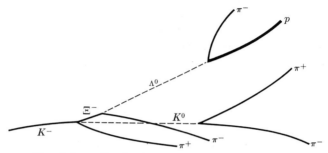

**Fig. 9.2** *Production of strange particles by kaons.*

followed by the slower decay processes

$$\Xi^- \rightarrow \Lambda^0 + \pi^- \tag{9.8}$$

$$\Lambda^0 \rightarrow p + \pi^- \tag{9.9}$$

$$\overline{K^0} \rightarrow \pi^+ + \pi^- \tag{9.10}$$

Strangeness is conserved in the initial production interaction but is violated in the three decay reactions. Note that the $\overline{K^0}$ antikaon decays into the same products as the $K^0$ kaon.

The behavior of kaons in their decay processes is quite different from that of any other particles. In Chap. 7 the alternate modes of decay of charged kaons into two pions or three pions were discussed [see Eq. (7.3)]; this was evidence for the violation of parity conservation in weak interactions.

The decay of the neutral $K^0$ and $\overline{K^0}$ kaons is even more unusual. They are also observed to decay into either two or three pions through two processes having greatly different half-lives of $0.7 \times 10^{-10}$ and $4 \times 10^{-8}$ sec. The two-pion decays for the $K^0$ and the $\overline{K^0}$ kaon can be written

$$K^0 \rightarrow \pi^+ + \pi^- \qquad \text{or} \qquad K^0 \rightarrow \pi^0 + \pi^0 \qquad (9.11)$$

and $\overline{K^0} \rightarrow \pi^- + \pi^+ \qquad \text{or} \qquad \overline{K^0} \rightarrow \pi^0 + \pi^0$

The decay products of the two $K^0$ particles are identical, and the probabilities or decay lifetimes should be the same. The three-pion decay processes for the two particles are

$$K^0 \rightarrow \pi^+ + \pi^- + \pi^0 \qquad (9.12)$$

$$\overline{K^0} \rightarrow \pi^- + \pi^+ + \pi^0$$

Here also the decay products are identical, and the lifetimes for decay should be the same.

In an attempt to understand this complexity in the decays, A. Pais and M. Gell-Mann proposed that the $K^0$ and $\overline{K^0}$ exist in a state with an equal probability of having $S = +1$ and $S = -1$. The quantum-mechanical description of such a combined state has two terms which can be combined as either a sum or a difference. In these two combinations the probability for decay into two pions is either enhanced or canceled. Such a combined state has a probability of decay which oscillates, through virtual processes involving the common $\pi^+$, $\pi^-$ products, between being a $K^0$ or a $\overline{K^0}$. The decay states, which are combinations of the creation states, are given different symbols. The constructive-interference state which has a high probability for decay into a pion pair is given the symbol $K^0_1$; the state for which the probabilities cancel is given the symbol $K^0_2$. The decay lifetime for the $K^0_1$ is relatively fast, $0.7 \times 10^{-10}$ sec. For the $K^0_2$ the decay into pion pairs is forbidden; so the state survives until it decays through the more complicated and lower probability process resulting in three pions with a longer lifetime of $4 \times 10^{-8}$ sec.

The explanation above seems to represent the observations. This unusual resonance behavior means that once either a $K^0$ or a $\overline{K^0}$ is formed, there is a 50 percent probability that it will decay in either the $K_1^0$ mode or the $K_2^0$ mode.   A $K^0$ beam, from either source, will rapidly turn into a $K_2^0$ beam as the $K_1^0$ dies out with the short-lived two-pion decay.   The $K_2^0$ beam, in the absence of matter, decays into three pions with the longer lifetime.   These properties of the $K^0$ kaons are illustrated schematically in Fig. 9.3, in which the fast decays of the $K_1^0$ and the slower decays of the

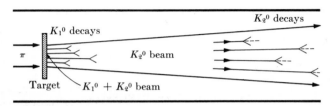

**Fig. 9.3**     *Illustration of the double decay of a $K^\circ$ beam.*

$K_2^0$ along an evacuated beam pipe are indicated.   This technique provides a mechanism for separating the $K_2^0$ beam for experimental studies.

However, in nuclear collisions the $K_2^0$ can act as though it has either positive or negative strangeness, since it can be described as a combination of $K^0$ and $\overline{K^0}$ states.   Both the $K_1^0$ and the $K_2^0$ can have nuclear interactions in matter which result in producing the $\Lambda^0$ which has $S = -1$ or, alternatively, both can produce the $\overline{\Lambda^0}$ which has $S = +1$.

### HYPERCHARGE

An alternate terminolgy for the strangeness selection rule has been proposed by G. F. Chew, M. Gell-Mann, and A. H. Rosenfeld. In this terminology the quantum-number *hypercharge Y* is used in place of strangeness $S$.   Hypercharge is twice (simply to make it integral) the average charge of a particle charge multiplet. Average charge $\bar{q}$ is just what the name implies, the numerical average of the electric charges of the multiplet.   The average charge $\bar{q}$ for a triplet state $(+q,0,-q)$ is 0, so $Y = 0$; that for a neutral singlet is also 0; for the nucleon doublet $\bar{q} = \frac{1}{2}$ and $Y = 1$; etc.  For mesons the hypercharge is the same as the strangeness number.  For baryons $Y = S + A$, where $A$ is the baryon number.

The relationships between isotopic spin, multiplicity of charge states, average charge, hypercharge, strangeness, and baryon number for hadrons are overspecified.  Selection of three of these quantum numbers will give the full amount of information.  The three used in this new terminology are baryon number $A$, isotopic spin $I$, and hypercharge $Y$.  With these the particle can be specified as to whether it is a baryon or meson, the multiplicity of charge states, and the degree of strangeness.  The values of the quantum numbers $A$, $I$, and $Y$ for the ten classes of strongly interacting particles which share the strangeness property are tabulated in Table 3.  For completeness, the multiplicity $M$ and strangeness $S$ are also given, although these properties are not needed when using this new terminology.

All of the strongly interacting particles listed in Table 2 fall into one or another of the families of states defined in Table 3.

**TABLE 3     Strangeness Quantum Numbers for Hadrons**

| NAME OF STATE | SYMBOL | BARYON NUMBER $A$ | ISOTOPIC SPIN $I$ | HYPER-CHARGE $Y$ | MULTI-PLICITY $M$ | STRANGE-NESS $S$ |
|---|---|---|---|---|---|---|
| Pion | $\pi$ | 0 | 1 | 0 | 3 | 0 |
| Kaon | $K$ | 0 | $\frac{1}{2}$ | +1 | 2 | +1 |
| Antikaon | $\bar{K}$ | 0 | $\frac{1}{2}$ | −1 | 2 | −1 |
| Eta | $\eta$ | 0 | 0 | 0 | 1 | 0 |
| Nucleon | $N$ | 1 | $\frac{1}{2}$ | +1 | 2 | 0 |
| N-star | $N_1^*$ | 1 | $\frac{3}{2}$ | +1 | 4 | 0 |
| Lambda | $\Lambda$ | 1 | 0 | 0 | 1 | −1 |
| Sigma | $\Sigma$ | 1 | 1 | 0 | 3 | −1 |
| Xi | $\Xi$ | 1 | $\frac{1}{2}$ | −1 | 2 | −2 |
| Omega | $\Omega$ | 1 | 0 | −2 | 1 | −3 |

Furthermore, as far as is known at present, all of the resonances discussed in Chap. 10 fall into one or another of these same families, but in general they have larger values for the spin quantum number $s$. In fact, one of these resonance states ($N_1^*$, with $s = \frac{3}{2}$), which does not exist as an identifiable particle and is not listed in Table 2, is included in Table 3 for completeness. Further discussion of the significance of these ten families of states listed in Table 3 is deferred until Chap. 12.

This alternate terminology using hypercharge rather than strangeness has been adopted by some other high-energy physicists in recent research publications. However, rather than confuse readers with these additional symbols and concepts, the earlier terminology using strangeness and isotopic spin has been retained throughout this survey.

*chapter 10*

# RESONANCES

THE NAME RESONANCE IS APPLIED to a large number of particle states with mass values greater than, and lifetimes shorter than, those of the "observable" particles listed in Table 2.

According to present concepts, the nucleon is a complex particle which can be described, for some purposes, as a core surrounded by a cloud of mesons. This concept is analogous to that for the atom in which a cloud of electrons surrounds the nucleus. Atomic structure studies have shown that the atom can have excited states in which electrons temporarily occupy higher-energy states. Each such excited state has a unique value of excitation energy; when the atoms return to the ground state these energy differences are radiated as photons which constitute the atomic spectra. Similarly, we might expect the mesonic cloud surrounding a nucleon core to be capable of existing in excited states of higher energy (and so of higher mass) and to "radiate" mesons.

The particle states known as resonances can be conceived as excitation states of one of the more stable particles. They can also be conceived as temporary compound states of a system constituting several strongly interacting particles or as particles similar to the observable particles, which are unstable against strong nuclear decay and so have extremely short lifetimes.

## EXPERIMENTAL METHODS

Evidence for the existence of resonances comes from several types of experimental studies. One type is the *excitation function* which is a plot of the yield of products from a particle interaction as a function of bombarding energy. In atomic and nuclear physics similar excitation function studies also show peaks which are called resonances; this name has been appropriated and applied to the same type of phenomenon in particle physics. In such a plot, broad peaks are frequently observed centered about specific values of energy. Such a preferred value of energy indicates a state of the system of two particles for which decay into the final products is more probable than for lower or higher values of the total excitation energy. When such a compound state decays, the product particles have considerable kinetic energy. The total excitation, or total mass, of the compound state can be calculated on the assumption of mass-energy conservation, from the sum of the rest masses and kinetic energies of either the initial or the product particles (with proper attention to the CM velocity due to conservation of momentum).

As an example, when beams of pions of known and controllable energy became available from high-energy accelerators, they were used as bombarding particles for scattering experiments. The total cross section (or yield) of pions elastically scattered from protons (using liquid-hydrogen targets) has been studied over a wide range of pion energy. With positive pions, when the yield is plotted as a function of pion energy, a single broad resonance peak is observed at pion energies of about 180 MeV (see Fig. 8.1). The scattering process can be written

$$\pi^+ + p \to N^* \to \pi^+ + p \tag{10.1}$$

Here the intermediate state $N^*$ is conceived to be an excited state of the proton-pion $(p,\pi)$ system with a mass determined by the energy of the resonance peak. Kinematic analysis shows the rest mass of this state to be 1238 MeV. This scattering process was also discussed in Chap. 8, where it was shown that conservation of isotopic spin leads to a value for this state of $I = \frac{3}{2}$. Further analysis shows its charge to be $+2q$, the spin to be $\frac{3}{2}$, and the parity even $(+)$. The current notation for describing this resonance is $N_1^*$ (1238, $\frac{3}{2}^+$).

When negative pions are scattered from protons a resonance peak is observed for the same incident energy of 180 MeV, also illustrated in Fig. 8.1. The scattering process is

$$\pi^- + p \rightarrow N^* \rightarrow \pi^- + p \tag{10.2}$$

The observation that the same resonance is produced with both positive and negative pions is strong evidence for the charge independence of nuclear forces. The state resulting from this interaction has neutral charge ($I_3 = -\frac{1}{2}$).

When pions of higher energy became available, these scattering studies were extended to higher energies; the cross sections showed another, smaller peak for $\pi^+$ at about 1.5 GeV and two additional peaks for $\pi^-$ at 600 and 900 MeV. These peaks represent other resonances of the $(p,\pi)$ system at still higher energies, having larger mass values and different spin states (see Fig. 8.1).

Another experimental technique is that of inelastic scattering. When a proton beam of fixed energy is used to bombard a proton target (liquid hydrogen), and the scattered protons emerging at a particular angle are momentum-analyzed by a magnetic field, those which are elastically scattered form a strong and sharp peak on a plot of yield versus magnetic field. However, the plot will in general also show several lesser peaks at lower values of magnetic field (see Fig. 10.1). These "inelastic" peaks are evidence of excitation states in the target proton which have mass values greater than the proton ground state. Again using $N^*$ to represent the excited particle, we can write

$$p + p \rightarrow N^* + p \tag{10.3}$$

This $N^*$ will decay quite promptly into product particles which might be, in this case,

$$N^* \rightarrow p + \pi^0 \quad \text{or} \quad N^* \rightarrow n + \pi^+ \tag{10.4}$$

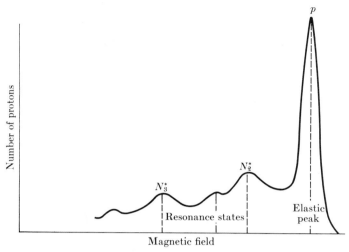

**Fig. 10.1**   *Resonances observed in inelastic scattering.*

Such an excited state differs from the ground state of the nucleon in some fundamental way.   The properties which can differ are intrinsic spin, parity, isotopic spin, strangeness, and rest mass.

The mass values of the $N^*$ states associated with inelastic peaks can be obtained by kinematic analysis of the scattering process.   The two strongest peaks observed in $p$-$p$ scattering indicate states for which the mass values are 1512 and 1688 MeV. Studies of the angular distributions of the protons associated with these inelastic peaks and application of parity conservation are used to determine the spins and parities, which are found to be $\frac{3}{2}^-$ and $\frac{5}{2}^+$, respectively.   These two resonances are designated by $N_2^*$ (1512, $\frac{3}{2}^-$) and $N_3^*$ (1688, $\frac{5}{2}^+$).

Still another procedure is to study the products of interactions which lead to product particles different from the incident ones.   One example is the charge exchange process

$$\pi^- + p \rightarrow X^{0*} + n \qquad\qquad (10.5)$$

where the unknown product $X^{0*}$ is a neutral mesonic state which decays promptly into lighter mesons. The product neutrons are emitted in several groups with different energies and velocities; time-of-flight techniques can be used to separate the groups. Electronic-coincidence techniques can be used to identify one group of neutrons as the products of a particular $X^{0*}$ state; kinematic analysis of the momenta and energies can then be used to determine the mass value of that state. For example, the $X^{0*}$ state might emit three pions, but its mass might be greater than that of three pions; this mass difference, with other information, can be used to determine the properties of the unknown resonance, which in this case is named the $\omega^0$ (785, $1^-$) resonance.

The detailed kinematic analysis of all products of a multi-product interaction can often lead to identification of a resonance state. Consider, for example, antiproton-proton annihilation resulting in several pairs of charged pions and one or more neutral pions

$$\overline{p^-} + p \rightarrow \pi^+ + \pi^+ + \underbrace{\pi^- + \pi^- + \pi^0}_{\omega^0} \qquad (10.6)$$

This process is illustrated in Fig. 10.2. The bubble-chamber photograph will show four charged pion tracks originating from the termination of the $\overline{p^-}$ track. Kinematic analysis of their momenta and energies shows that there must be at least one additional $\pi^0$ pion emitted and defines its direction and energy. Further analysis shows that a group of three pions must have been emitted in the form of a single mesonic particle (the $\omega^0$ resonance mentioned above), which then promptly decays into three separate pions. The sum of the rest masses and energies of the three pions determine the mass energy of the $\omega^0$ resonance. This intermediate resonance is illustrated in Fig. 10.2 in a highly magnified and imaginary view of this two-step interaction.

Still another example of a resonance determined through kinematic or "missing mass" analysis is the $\Lambda^0$ production reaction

$$\pi^- + p \rightarrow \Lambda^0 + K^0 + \pi^0 \qquad (10.7)$$

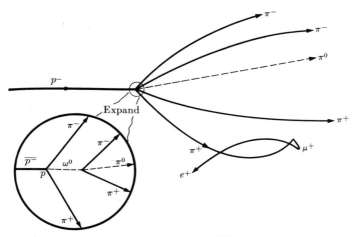

**Fig. 10.2** *Annihilation interaction,* $\overline{p^-} + p \to$ *mesons, showing temporary formation of an* $\omega^\circ$ *resonance state.*

This could also be a two-step process

$$\pi^- + p \to \Lambda^{0*} + K^0$$

followed by

$$\Lambda^{0*} \to \Lambda^0 + \pi^0 \tag{10.8}$$

The three neutral final products can all be observed and identified through their specific decay processes or "signatures"

$$\Lambda^0 \to p + \pi^- \qquad (T = 1.8 \times 10^{-10} \text{ sec})$$

$$K^0 \to \pi^+ + \pi^- \qquad (T = 0.7 \times 10^{-10} \text{ sec}) \tag{10.9}$$

$$\pi^0 \to \gamma + \gamma \qquad (T = 0.7 \times 10^{-16} \text{ sec})$$

In a two-particle decay such as Eq. (10.8), conservation of energy and momentum requires that the two products have unique values of energy; in a three-particle decay such as Eq. (10.7), each particle has a broad spread of energies. From statistical studies and plots of the observed energies of the products, the conclusion has been reached that in a large number of instances the process goes through two steps as in Eq. (10.8). This conclusion allows the mass of the $\Lambda^{0*}$ resonance to be determined. In present terminology this is the $Y_0^*$ (1815, $\frac{5}{2}+$) resonance.

The same resonance can often be produced through two or more alternate production processes. For example, the $N_2^*$ resonance is observed in inelastic electron scattering, which proceeds through the electromagnetic interaction

$$e + p \rightarrow N_2^* + e' \tag{10.10}$$

where the $e'$ peak has lower energy than the elastic peak. The excited nucleon state will decay promptly into a proton plus neutral pion or into a neutron plus positive pion [see Eq. (10.4)]. The same resonance can be produced with high-energy photons (photoproduction) on deuterium, which is also an electromagnetic interaction

$$\gamma + d \rightarrow N_2^* + n \tag{10.11}$$

The masses and other properties for many resonances are well established. By 1967 over 60 states which decay through the strong nuclear interaction had been identified, in addition to the "observable" particles listed in Table 2 which decay through electromagnetic or weak interactions and have longer lifetimes. Many more resonances have been reported for which the evidence is less complete. The similarity of this spectrum of resonances to the excited states observed in atomic and nuclear physics suggests that other states of still higher excitation can be anticipated, as the energies from accelerators increase and additional experimental techniques are developed. A list of some of the best-established resonances with their masses and other properties is given in Table 4. This list is far from complete and

**TABLE 4    Some Resonances, or Particle States, Decaying through the Strong Interaction**

| SYMBOL | MASS, MeV | WIDTH, MeV | SPIN | PARITY | ISOTOPIC SPIN | STRANGE-NESS | BARYON NUMBER |
|---|---|---|---|---|---|---|---|
| $\eta^0$ | 548 | <10 | 0 | $-1$ | 0 | 0 | 0 |
| $\rho^0$ | 750 | 100 | 1 | $-1$ | 1 | 0 | 0 |
| $\omega^0$ | 785 | <20 | 1 | $-1$ | 0 | 0 | 0 |
| $K^*$ | 890 | 50 | 1 | $-1$ | $\frac{1}{2}$ | $\pm 1$ | 0 |
| $N_1^*$ | 1238 | 150 | $\frac{3}{2}$ | $+1$ | $\frac{3}{2}$ | 0 | 1 |
| $N_2^*$ | 1512 | 130 | $\frac{3}{2}$ | $-1$ | $\frac{1}{2}$ | 0 | 1 |
| $N_3^*$ | 1690 | 140 | $\frac{5}{2}$ | $+1$ | $\frac{1}{2}$ | 0 | 1 |
| $N_4^*$ | 1920 | 185 | $\frac{9}{2}$? | $+1$ | $\frac{1}{2}$ | 0 | 1 |
| $Y_1^*$ | 1385 | 50 | $\frac{3}{2}$ | $+1$ | 1 | $-1$ | 1 |
| $Y_0^*$ | 1405 | 100 | $\frac{1}{2}$ | $-1$ | 0 | $-1$ | 1 |
| $Y_0^*$ | 1520 | 16 | $\frac{3}{2}$ | $-1$ | 0 | $-1$ | 1 |
| $Y_0^*$ | 1815 | 200 | $\frac{5}{2}$ | $+1$ | 0 | $-1$ | 1 |
| $\Xi^*$ | 1530 | $\sim$10 | $\frac{3}{2}$ | $+1$ | $\frac{1}{2}$ | $-2$ | 1 |

is intended only to illustrate the general characteristics of resonances.

## LIFETIMES AND WIDTHS

The *width* of an energy level is a quantum-mechanical concept arising through the Heisenberg uncertainty principle (see Chap. 3), which defines the limit to the uncertainties in the simultaneous determination of energy $\Delta E$ and of time $\Delta t$

$$\Delta E \, \Delta t \sim h \qquad (10.12)$$

When this limit is inserted in the mathematical expression describing the wave function of the state, $\Psi(x,y,z,it)$, and the probability of survival of the wave function after a time $t$ is computed, $\Psi\Psi^*$, it is found to be proportional to $e^{-2\pi\Gamma t/h}$, where $\Gamma$ is defined as the energy width of the state. The quantity $2\pi\Gamma/h$ is the probability of decay per unit time, or the reciprocal of the mean life $\tau$ of the state. Mean life is defined as the time for the population of the state to be reduced to $1/e$ of its initial value. So the energy width is related to the mean life as

$$\Gamma \tau = \frac{h}{2\pi} \qquad (10.13)$$

This means that, because of the finite lifetime of an excited state, the energy of the state cannot be sharply defined but is indeterminate within the energy spread $\Gamma$. Inserting the numerical value of $h$, we have

$$\tau = \frac{0.66 \times 10^{-21}}{\Gamma \text{ (MeV)}} \text{ sec} \qquad (10.14)$$

It has not been found possible to measure both $\Gamma$ and $\tau$ for the same state, because $h$ is so small. For states in which the lifetime is long enough to measure, such as the particles in Table 2, this relation can be used to compute the energy width of the state; for example, if the lifetime is $10^{-10}$ sec, the width is about $10^{-5}$ eV. In Table 2, lifetimes are reported in the form of the half-life $T$, which is the time for half of the particles to decay. The mean lifetime $\tau$, which is the time to decay to $1/e$ of the initial population, is related as $\tau = 1.44 \ T$.

For the resonances, where the lifetimes are too short to be measured, they can be computed from measured values of the widths, using Eq. (10.14). Experimentally, most of the resonance peaks observed in excitation functions or in inelastic scattering are observed to have broad natural widths. The method of measuring the width is to determine and subtract the base level (or background) under the peak, through whatever information is available, and then to measure the full width of the resulting symmetrical peak at $1/e$ of its height. The base level is usually obvious from the general trend of the plot on which the peaks are superimposed. If two levels overlap, they can be separated by subtraction. If a resonance peak is unsymmetrical, it can often be resolved into two overlapping peaks representing two resonances.

In Table 4 the measured widths of some of the best-established of the resonances are listed, in million electron volts, alongside their masses. The $\eta^0$ resonance has such a narrow width that its lifetime is quite long compared with other strong interactions (estimated $\sim 10^{-16}$ sec); because of this relatively long life it is usually included in the tabulations of the observable particles and is so included in Table 2. Many of these resonances have natural widths which are 5 to 10 percent of their total mass-energy values. For a state with a width of 200 MeV, the lifetime computed from Eq. (10.14) is only $3.3 \times 10^{-22}$ sec. If we consider a nucleon to have a diameter of about $3 \times 10^{-13}$ cm, this state survives for a time only long enough for a particle at the velocity of light to traverse a distance of a few hundred nucleon diameters from the point of the interaction. These are indeed short-lived states.

## BARYON RESONANCES

Resonances fall into two clearly separable categories, those with masses greater than nucleons, which decay into nucleons, and those whose decay products are other mesons. Baryon resonances have baryon numbers $\pm 1$, while meson resonances have baryon number 0.

V. F. Weisskopf* has summarized the spectrum of baryon resonances in a diagram which is redrawn and presented as Fig. 10.3. In this figure the best-known baryon resonances are plotted on a vertical scale of mass in GeV units and separated into six families distinguished by different values of strangeness and isotopic number. The baryons listed in Table 2 appear as the *ground states* of the several families of resonances. The multiplicity of charge states is indicated for each family by the

* *Science*, 149, Sept. 10, 1965.

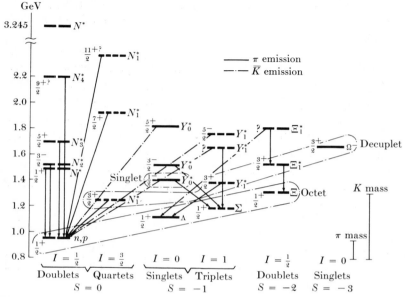

**Fig. 10.3**  *Spectrum of the energy states of the baryon. The isotopic spin I and the strangeness S are given at the bottom, the angular spin and parity are given at the left of the level, the symbol at the right. The isotopic multiplicity, the transitions by meson emission, and some SU(3) multiplets are indicated. (Courtesy of V. F. Weisskopf.)*

number of members of approximately equal mass; the charge of individual particles is not shown. The symbols designating the state, and the spin and parity assignments, are indicated for the several members of each family, where known. For clarity, this spectrum includes only the particles; an equivalent spectrum of antiparticles probably exists with reversed signs for the strangeness number. Presumably for each particle state or resonance there is an antiparticle state, but experimental evidence for the antibaryon spectrum is scanty. One additional state has been added to Weisskopf's spectrum, the $N^*$ (3245) resonance, reported from the Argonne Laboratory in 1966.

## MESON RESONANCES

The spectrum of meson resonances is presented in Fig. 10.4, also adapted from Weisskopf's summary of 1965. The mesons and their known resonances listed in Table 2 are plotted on a mass scale in million electron volts, separated into four families with different values of strangeness and isotopic number. Charge multiplicity is indicated in each family, but the charge of individual states is not shown. Values of spin and parity are noted, where known. In this spectrum, both the kaons and the antikaons are included for completeness; the antikaons have a strangeness number of $-1$.

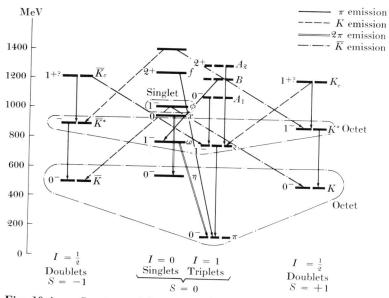

**Fig. 10.4**    *Spectrum of the energy states of the meson. Isotopic spin I and strangeness S are given at the bottom, angular spin and parity at the left of the level, the symbol at the right. The isotopic multiplicity, the transitions by meson emission, and some SU(3) multiplets are indicated. (Courtesy of V. F. Weisskopf.)*

A large fraction of our present information on the mass energies and other properties of the excited particle states called resonances is illustrated in Figs. 10.3 and 10.4.   For most of the states pictured in the figures the modes of decay are known or assumed, involving the emission of pions or kaons.   These are illustrated in Weisskopf's presentation by solid or dotted lines leading from an upper state to a lower one and identified as to their type.   The properties of particle states illustrated in these two figures are the source material for theoretical analysis and correlations.   Some of the theoretical approaches toward correlation are discussed briefly in Chap. 12.

*chapter 11*

# EXERCISES
# IN CONSERVATION

IN THE ANALYSIS OF EXPERIMENTAL results, the basic task is to apply the conservation principles which are pertinent to the interaction under study. It is not essential that all conservation laws be analyzed and confirmed in every experiment. But a useful experiment will provide sufficient information and adequate precision to evaluate those properties which are to be tested. In most experiments some of the basic conservation laws are taken for granted and are not checked in detail. The conservation of mass energy is so well established through thousands of past observations that it is hardly necessary to reconfirm the principle in an experiment planned, for example, to analyze particle spins. On the other hand, an experiment should be designed to allow the analysis of as many properties which can be checked by conservation laws as possible to provide the widest possible evidence for a possible new phenomenon.

When the evidence from an experiment suggests the existence of a new particle or resonance state, the unknown properties of this state can usually be determined by applying the known conservation laws. If the evidence seems to violate a known conservation law, the first responsibility is to restudy the interpretation of results to avoid an erroneous conclusion. When all possible checks have been applied and the evidence still violates some conservation principle, the need for a new and broader conservation principle may be indicated. For example, the unusual properties of the strange particles which violated earlier concepts led to the new principle of conservation of strangeness.

To illustrate the use of conservation principles we shall analyze in this chapter some basic and typical interactions to demonstrate either conservation or violation and to show what conclusions can be drawn. We shall select examples which illustrate separately the three interactions involving particles:

the strong, electromagnetic, and weak interactions. We start
with simple processes in which only the incident and final particle states are considered. Then we extend the illustrations
to more complex interactions involving resonance states and
sequential decay processes.

### SUMMARY OF CONSERVATION LAWS

The conservation laws of physics identify certain qualities or
properties of matter which do not change during interactions.

**TABLE 5      Conservation Laws**

| | NAME | CONSERVATION PRINCIPLE | INTERACTIONS | | |
|---|---|---|---|---|---|
| | | | Strong | Electro-mag-netic | Weak |
| 1 | *Energy* | $\Sigma(T + m_0c^2) = $ const (numerical sum) | Yes | Yes | Yes |
| 2 | *Linear momentum* | $\Sigma(m\mathbf{v}) = $ const (vector sum) | Yes | Yes | Yes |
| 3 | *Angular momentum* | $\Sigma(m\mathbf{v}) \times \mathbf{r} = $ const (vector sum) or $\Sigma\mathbf{j} = $ const (vector sum) | Yes | Yes | Yes |
| 4 | *Charge* | $\Sigma(q) = $ const (algebraic sum) | Yes | Yes | Yes |
| 5 | *Particle number* | $\Sigma(A) = $ const (algebraic sum) $\Sigma(N_e) = $ const (algebraic sum) $\Sigma(N\mu) = $ const (algebraic sum) | Yes — — | Yes Yes Yes | Yes Yes Yes |
| 6 | *Parity* | $\Pi(P(-1)^l) = $ const (algebraic product) | Yes | Yes | No |
| 7 | *Isotopic spin* | $\Sigma(I) = $ const (vector sum) $\Sigma(I_3) = $ const (algebraic sum) | Yes Yes | No Yes | No No |
| 8 | *Strangeness* | $\Sigma(S) = $ const (algebraic sum) | Yes | Yes | No |

The eight conservation principles described in the preceding chapters summarize essentially all our experimental evidence on the properties of particles and their interactions. These eight conservation laws are listed with a concise symbolic representation of each conservation principle in Table 5. The types of particle interactions for which these conservation laws are valid are also indicated in the table. The first five of the conservation laws listed are valid for all interactions in nature, so far as we know, including all particle and antiparticle interactions. The last three have a narrower range of validity, but they are all conserved in strong interactions and violated in weak interactions. Isotopic spin is the only one violated in electromagnetic interactions. The techniques used for identifying the conserved qualities and for applying the conservation principles will become evident in the illustrations which follow. In general, whatever can happen without violating a conservation law does happen.

### STRONG INTERACTIONS

The strong interaction involves the nuclear force which binds protons and neutrons in nuclei. It is responsible for interactions between baryons and mesons and for the creation of mesons. When a strong interaction is "allowed," in the sense that it obeys all eight of the conservation laws, it goes extremely fast, in times of the order of $10^{-22}$ sec. When it is "forbidden," when one or more of the conservation laws is violated, it is possible that an electromagnetic or a weak interaction can occur. Evidence that a strong interaction is forbidden comes either from failure to observe it in any instance or from the observation that the process has a relatively much longer lifetime than other fast interactions.

A basic interaction is the elastic scattering of high-energy protons by protons

$$p + p \rightarrow p + p \qquad (11.1)$$

Many experiments show, when the dynamics of the interaction are analyzed, that energy and momentum are conserved. Angular momentum **j** is conserved if the vector sum of intrinsic spins plus orbital angular momenta remains the same. A quantum-mechanical analysis of the allowed orientations of **s** and **l** can be used to predict the angular distribution of the products. As to other quantum numbers, since incident and product particles are identical, the charge $q$, particle number $A$, isotopic spin $I$, and strangeness $S$ quantum numbers are all obviously conserved. This is clearly an "allowed" strong interaction.

Another basic interaction is the scattering of protons by neutrons

$$p + n \rightarrow p + n \tag{11.2}$$

Here, also, energy, momentum, and the quantum numbers $q$, $A$, $I$, and $S$ can obviously be conserved. The difference is in the way in which angular momentum is conserved, which involves the application of Pauli's exclusion principle. For example, in proton-proton scattering [Eq. (11.1)] the incoming proton and the target proton cannot interact if their spins are parallel but interact only if they are antiparallel. In proton-neutron scattering, however, this exclusion does not exist since they are different particles; scattering can occur from either of the two opposed spin states of the neutron. A simplified visualization of these spin orientations is illustrated in Fig. 11.1. The angular distributions observed for $p$-$p$ and $p$-$n$ scattering are different, even though both involve orbital angular momenta in addition to spin. The difference observed in these angular distributions is consistent with the application of the Pauli exclusion principle described above.

Consider next the capture of $\pi^-$ pions by deuterons; this reaction was discussed earlier in Chap. 7. We can assume that energy and linear momentum are conserved, although this could

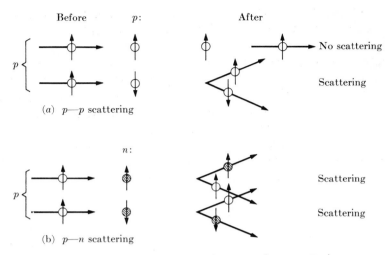

**Fig. 11.1** *Spin orientations in p-p and p-n scattering.*

be verified by experimental measurement of neutron properties. In this case we present the remaining quantum numbers and conserved quantities in tabular form:

$$\pi^- + d \rightarrow \quad n + n \qquad (11.3)$$

Angular momentum $j$: $\quad 0 \ + l = \quad \frac{1}{2} + \frac{1}{2} + l$

Charge $\qquad\qquad q$: $-1 \ + 1 = \quad 0 + 0$

Number $\qquad\qquad A$: $\quad 0 \ + 2 = \quad 1 + 1$

Parity $\qquad\qquad P$: $-1 \ \times 1 = \quad 1 \times 1 \times (l)^{-1}$

Isotopic spin $\qquad I$: $\quad 1 \ + 0 = \quad \frac{1}{2} + \frac{1}{2}$

$\qquad\qquad\qquad\quad I_3$: $-1 \ + 0 = -\frac{1}{2} - \frac{1}{2}$

Strangeness $\qquad S$: $\quad 0 \ + 0 = \quad 0 + 0$

All seven of the quantum numbers above are conserved. The angular-momentum balance above is only symbolic, since the vector sum of all terms including spin and orbital momentum must be included. We note that the requirement discussed in Chap. 7 for the two neutrons to be emitted in different states with relative angular momentum introduces another odd term in the parity balance; this, in fact, was used to determine the parity of the $\pi^-$ pion. We can conclude that this interaction is allowed and should have a large yield, which is in agreement with observations.

A possible alternative process in the capture of $\pi^-$ pions by deuterons is

$$\pi^- + d \xrightarrow{?} n + \pi^0 \qquad (11.4)$$

$A: \quad 0 + 2 \neq 1 + 0$

$I: \quad 1 + 0 \neq \frac{1}{2} + 1$

$I_3: -1 + 0 \neq -\frac{1}{2} + 0$

Although other conservation laws might be obeyed, it is clear that, at least for particle number and isotopic spin, the conservation laws are violated and the process is forbidden. It is not observed.

In the annihilation of antiprotons with protons the dominant process is the production of many pions, already described in Eq. (10.6) and illustrated in Fig. 10.2. The total mass energy of the proton-antiproton pair (1.876 GeV) plus the incoming kinetic energy is distributed between the rest masses and kinetic energies of charged and neutral pions. A typical reaction might be

$$\overline{p^-} + p^+ \rightarrow \pi^+ + \pi^- + \pi^+ + \pi^- + \pi^0 \qquad (11.5)$$

$j: \quad \frac{1}{2} + \frac{1}{2} = 0 + 0 + 0 + 0 + 0 + l$

$q: -1 + 1 = 1 - 1 + 1 - 1 + 0$

$A: -1 + 1 = 0 + 0 + 0 + 0 + 0$

$P: +1 \times +1 = -1 \times -1 \times -1 \times -1 \times -1 \times (l)^{-1}$

$I_3: -\frac{1}{2} + \frac{1}{2} = 1 + -1 + 1 + -1 + 0$

$S: -1 + 1 = 0 + 0 + 0 + 0 + 0$

All six of the quantum numbers above are conserved. The number of pairs of charged pions does not affect the conservation balance but is determined by the available energy. If another $\pi^0$ pion is emitted, it will be associated with the other pions with relative angular momentum, so parity can still be conserved.

The annihilation process above may also proceed in two steps involving the temporary formation of an $\omega^0$ resonance, illustrated in the insert in Fig. 10.2. The properties of the $\omega^0$ resonance can be studied by applying the conservation laws in two steps. First consider the initial production process

$$\overline{p} + p \quad \rightarrow \quad \pi^+ + \quad \pi^- + \omega^0 \qquad (11.6)$$

$$j: \quad \tfrac{1}{2} + \quad \tfrac{1}{2} + l \quad = \quad 0 + \quad 0 + ?; \text{ so } \ s = \quad 1 \text{ for } \omega^0$$

$$q: -1 + \quad 1 \quad = \quad 0 + \quad 0 + ?; \text{ so } \ q = \quad 0 \text{ for } \omega^0$$

$$A: -1 + \quad 1 \quad = \quad 0 + \quad 0 + ?; \text{ so } A = \quad 0 \text{ for } \omega^0$$

$$P: +1 \ \times +1 \times (l)^{-1} = \ -1 \ \times -1 \ \times \ ?; \text{ so } P = -1 \text{ for } \omega^0$$

$$I_3: -\tfrac{1}{2} + \quad \tfrac{1}{2} \quad = \quad 1 + -1 \ + ?; \text{ so } I_3 = \quad 0 \text{ for } \omega^0$$

$$S: -1 + \quad 1 \quad = \quad 0 + \quad 0 + ?; \text{ so } S = \quad 0 \text{ for } \omega^0$$

The identifications of $s = 1$ and $P = -1$ for the $\omega^0$ above are symbolic; detailed analysis involves a more complicated procedure. Furthermore, we can assume that energy and momentum are conserved in this initial process and can identify the $\pi^+$, $\pi^-$, $\pi^0$ which are the ultimate products of the $\omega^0$; so we can determine the direction of the $\omega^0$ and its mass energy, which is 785 MeV.

Following its production, the $\omega^0$ breaks up into three pions

$$\omega^0 \rightarrow \pi^+ + \pi^- + \pi^0 \qquad (11.7)$$

Using the values above for the properties and quantum numbers of the $\omega^0$, we can analyze this process to show that all conservation laws are obeyed. This analysis provides the evidence for the existence of the $\omega^0$ resonance state to which has been given the symbol $\omega^0$ (785, 0$^-$).

Another, more complicated annihilation process, observed in a liquid-hydrogen bubble-chamber photograph at the CERN laboratory in Geneva, is illustrated in Fig. 11.2. Kinematic

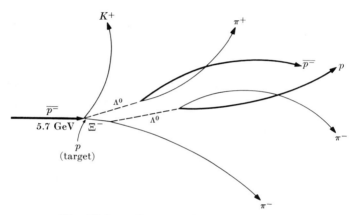

**Fig. 11.2**     *Proton-antiproton annihilation.*

analysis of the sequence of events, based on the observed track curvatures in the magnetic field, led to identification of each particle; the results are indicated by the symbols in the figure. The initial annihilation process produces three strange particles.

$$\overline{p} + p \rightarrow \Xi^- + \overline{\Lambda^0} + K^+ \tag{11.8}$$

In justification of these assignments, consider the two conservation laws pertinent to strong interactions:

Isotopic spin $I_3$: $-\frac{1}{2} + \frac{1}{2} = -\frac{1}{2} + 0 + \frac{1}{2}$; conserved

Strangeness $S$: $0 + 0 = -2 + 1 + 1$; conserved

The three products were identified through their decay processes

$$\Xi^- \to \Lambda^0 + \pi^- \tag{11.9}$$

followed by

$$\Lambda^0 \to p + \pi^- \tag{11.10}$$

and $\overline{\Lambda^0} \to \overline{p^-} + \pi^+$ (11.11)

and $K^+ \to \pi^+ + \pi^0$ (11.12)

If we apply the same two conservation laws to these decay processes we have

| ISOTOPIC SPIN $I_3$ | | | STRANGENESS $S$ | | | |
|---|---|---|---|---|---|---|
| $-\frac{1}{2}$ $\neq$ | $0$ | $-1$ | $-2$ $\neq$ | $-1$ | $+0$ | (11.9) |
| $0$ $\neq$ | $\frac{1}{2}$ | $-1$ | $-1$ $\neq$ | $0$ | $+0$ | (11.10) |
| $0$ $\neq$ | $-\frac{1}{2}$ | $+1$ | $1$ $\neq$ | $0$ | $+0$ | (11.11) |
| $\frac{1}{2}$ $\neq$ | $1$ | $+0$ | $1$ $\neq$ | $0$ | $+0$ | (11.12) |

Both conservation laws are violated for all four decay reactions. The conclusion is that these decays cannot be strong interactions, which is also justified by the observation of relatively long lifetimes for each.

### ELECTROMAGNETIC INTERACTIONS

The subject of many publications in scientific journals and textbooks, quantum electrodynamics is the theoretical framework which describes the interactions between the charges and magnetic moments of particles at rest and in motion. It is the modern form of the theory of electromagnetism to which have been added the principles of quantum mechanics and special relativity. Quantum electrodynamics was developed to explain the phenomena of atomic physics and has been extended with considerable success to nuclear physics.

Electromagnetic effects in particle physics are small compared with the strong nuclear interactions between particles.

The ratio of the strengths or coupling constants of the electromagnetic to the strong interactions is about $1:100$; it is of interest to note that this ratio is the same order as the atomic fine-structure constant, $2\pi e^2/hc = \frac{1}{137}$. For interactions between individual high-energy particles, the effect of charge is in general small as compared with that of the strong interaction and can be added as a small correction.

Quantum electrodynamics applies to essentially all high-energy phenomena involving the production or absorption of photons. Pions are produced through photoproduction processes of the type

$$\gamma + p \rightarrow n + \pi^+$$
$$\gamma + n \rightarrow p + \pi^-, \text{ etc.}$$

$(11.13)$

At higher photon energies, pions are produced in pairs, triples, or even larger numbers. In all such photoproduction processes, all conservation laws are obeyed except that for isotopic spin. This can be noted in the equations above, where $I = \frac{1}{2}$ for both protons and neutrons and $I = 1$ for pions; isotopic-spin conservation is violated. Yet, because all other conservation laws are obeyed, these photoproduction processes have a relatively large yield or cross section of about 1 percent of that for strong interactions.

Photoproduction processes can produce hyperons and other strange particles, if photon energies are sufficient to be above threshold for the process. The following are typical

$$\gamma + p \rightarrow \Lambda^0 + K^+$$
$$\gamma + p \rightarrow \Sigma^0 + K^+$$
$$\gamma + p \rightarrow \Sigma^+ + K^0$$
$$\gamma + p \rightarrow \Sigma^+ + K^+ + \pi^-$$
$$\gamma + p \rightarrow \Sigma^- + K^+ + \pi^+$$

$(11.14)$

Strangeness is conserved in all these processes, but isotopic-spin conservation is violated.

Processes leading to photon products are also, in general, electromagnetic interactions. One of the simplest is positron annihilation

$$e^+ + e^- \rightarrow \gamma + \gamma \qquad (11.15)$$

The fact that momentum and energy are conserved is demonstrated by many observations of the directions of the emergent photons and their energies. If the positron is at rest, the two photons emerge in opposite directions to conserve momentum, and each photon has an energy equal to the rest mass of an electron. Without going too deeply into electromagnetic theory, we can note that the sum of the two electron spins can be zero, and the sum of the two photon spins can also add to zero, vectorially. A more detailed justification of spin conservation must be left to the textbooks in electromagnetic theory. Since the positron is the antielectron, charge and particle number are conserved. The parity of a single free electron is even and that of a single photon is odd; when coupled in pairs as in this reaction, both the initial and final states are even and parity is conserved. Neither isotopic spin nor strangeness is involved in this reaction.

The decay of the $\pi^0$ pion into photons

$$\pi^0 \rightarrow \gamma + \gamma \qquad (11.16)$$

was discussed in Chap. 8, where it was shown that no isotopic-spin value could be assigned to the photon. The $\pi^0$ decays in flight, and its forward momentum and energy are transferred to the photons. Because of their momentum they form a symmetrical forward angle and can be detected through their electron-pair production process in matter. Since the spin of the pion is 0, and that of each photon is 1, spin can be conserved if the photon spins cancel. Charge is 0 and particle number is 0 for all particles involved; so charge and particle number are conserved. The parity of all three particles is odd; so parity is conserved only if the photons are emitted with relative angular momentum of $l = 1$, which requires a more detailed analysis of the electromagnetic process.

One process is known in which a heavy strange particle decays into another strange particle and a photon

$$\Sigma^0 \rightarrow \Lambda^0 + \gamma \qquad\qquad (11.17)$$

The evidence that this process is not a strong interaction is its relatively long lifetime of about $10^{-11}$ sec. The fact that the second product is a photon is reason for considering it an electromagnetic process. By applying analyses similar to those used in earlier examples, we can show that all conservation laws are obeyed except that of isotopic spin. The isotopic spin of the $\Sigma^0$ is 1, since the $\Sigma$ particle occurs in three charged states; that of the $\Lambda^0$ is 0, since it has only one charge state. So isotopic spin conservation is violated, and the process is forbidden as a strong interaction.

### WEAK INTERACTIONS

Weak interactions are associated with leptons and with the decay of baryons and mesons into leptons. They were first recognized in $\beta$-ray decay, where Fermi's early theory postulated the simultaneous emission of a neutrino with the $\beta$-ray electron to conserve energy, momentum, and spin. Weak interactions are involved in the decay of pions into muons, also with the emission of neutrinos.

When strong nuclear interactions are forbidden, through violation of some conservation law, the particle survives for a very long time on the nuclear time scale until the extremely weak forces of the weak nuclear interaction can cause a decay into lighter mass particles. We do not know the origin of this weak interaction or of the force which causes it. We do know that the strength of the coupling constant in weak interactions is about $10^{-13}$ of that applying in the strong interactions. And we know that many particles which are stable against strong interactions and electromagnetic interactions do decay eventually into lighter and more stable particles.

The most fundamental weak interaction is the decay of the free neutron into a proton, an electron, and an antineutrino

$$n \rightarrow p^+ + e^- + \overline{\nu_e} \qquad (T = 700 \text{ sec}) \qquad (11.18)$$

This process has been observed with thermal neutrons produced in a reactor, which decay in an ionization chamber where both of the charged products can be detected and identified. The electrons are emitted with a wide distribution in energy, indicating the simultaneous emission of the antineutrino to conserve energy, momentum, and spin in the process. Charge is conserved. Both baryon number and electron-family number are conserved when the neutrino is identified as an antineutrino. Conservation of parity, isotopic spin, and strangeness are all violated, which is typical of a weak interaction.

An even simpler example is the decay of charged pions into muons and muon neutrinos

$$\pi^+ \rightarrow \mu^+ + \overline{\nu_\mu} \qquad \text{and} \qquad \pi^- \rightarrow \overline{\mu^-} + \nu_\mu \qquad (11.19)$$

These processes can occur with the pions at rest in the absence of matter, in which case the mass difference $(m_\pi - m_\mu)$ is shared in the recoil energies of the muon and neutrino. It can also occur in flight with additional kinetic energy. The two products recoil in opposite directions and with spins opposed to conserve momentum and spin, as discussed in Chap. 7. Charge is obviously conserved. Muon number is conserved since one particle and one antiparticle result from each of the processes. Parity

and isotopic spin are not obeyed in this weak interaction; strangeness is not involved.

The decay of muons into electrons and two neutrinos follows the reactions

$$\overline{\mu^+} \rightarrow \overline{e^+} + \nu_e + \overline{\nu_\mu} \qquad \text{and} \qquad \mu^- \rightarrow e^- + \overline{\nu_e} + \nu_\mu \qquad (11.20)$$

The electrons emerge with a wide energy spread, indicating a three-body decay process. Although neutrino energies and momenta have not been measured, it is assumed that total energy and momentum are conserved. The vector sum of spins can be conserved if the spins of two of the product particles are opposed and cancel. Charge is conserved. Electron-family number and muon-family number are conserved in both processes when antiparticles with negative values are included. And, again, parity and isotopic spin conservation are violated.

The most common of the weak interactions is beta decay of radioactive nuclei; it is of two types, representing the transformation of a neutron in the nucleus into a proton and the reverse. The examples used in Chap. 7, which are typical, are

$$_{27}\text{Co}^{60} \rightarrow {}_{28}\text{Ni}^{60} + e^- + \overline{\nu_e} \qquad (11.21)$$

$$\text{and} \quad _{15}\text{P}^{30} \rightarrow {}_{14}\text{Si}^{30} + \overline{e^+} + \nu_e \qquad (11.22)$$

Although the nuclei are involved in the reactions and share in the recoil energy, momentum, and spin balances, as discussed in Chap. 7, we now assume that these properties are conserved. The total electric charge is conserved, as indicated by the atomic number change of the parent and product nuclei. The baryon number of the nucleus is unchanged; electron-family number is conserved with the emission of one particle and one antiparticle in each process.

Most of the principal decay modes of the observable particles in Table 2 represent weak interactions. Consider the decay of

the charged $K^+$ kaon in the two alternate processes discussed in Chap. 7, resulting in two or in three pion products

$$K^+ \rightarrow \pi^+ + \pi^0 \qquad\qquad (11.23)$$

and $K^+ \rightarrow \pi^+ + \pi^+ + \pi^-$

In the two-pion decay the $\pi^+$ is observed to have a single value of energy determined by the mass change and the incoming kaon energy, and the two pions recoil in opposite directions. On the other hand, in the three-pion process the products have a distribution in energy and direction, but again the total energy and momentum are conserved. The spin of all particles is zero, so spin is conserved. Electric charge is also conserved. Note that all particles are mesons, for which conservation of particle number does not apply. In Chap. 7 these alternative decay modes of the kaon were shown to lead to the breakdown of parity conservation; parity is not conserved in the two-pion process. Isotopic spin and strangeness conservation are both violated for both of the $K^+$ decay modes, which makes the strong interaction forbidden.

As a final example, consider the decay of the $\Omega^-$ hyperon

$$\Omega^- \rightarrow \Xi^- + K^0 + \pi^0 \qquad\qquad (11.24)$$

Only a few examples have been observed, in bubble chambers in which the charged particles resulting from the decay of the two neutral products have been measured and the process has been analyzed. The analysis assumes conservation of energy and momentum. The intrinsic spins of the particles are not conserved, so there must be relative angular momentum $l = 1$ in the process. Charge and particle number are both conserved. But conservation of parity, isotopic spin, and strangeness are all violated; so this must be a weak interaction.

*chapter 12*

# BASIC
# SYMMETRIES
# OF NATURE

IN OUR SEARCH FOR ORDER and system in nature we demonstrate our faith that the laws of nature are based on fundamental simplicities. Our past experience comes largely from the two most readily observable forces, gravitation and electromagnetism. To the first we ascribe the motions of planets and of falling bodies on our earth; the second describes all atomic and chemical processes and all electromagnetic phenomena. Both gravitational and electromagnetic forces vary inversely with the square of the distance between masses or between electric charges. This similarity has been of real value in aiding our understanding, through analogy, of phenomena involving the two kinds of force. We feel that it is "natural" for forces to vary with the inverse square of the distance.

Now we are faced with many new phenomena involving a nuclear force which has greatly different properties. This force is extremely strong at the spacings of nucleons in nuclei and falls off very rapidly with distance so that it is negligible at spacings of a few nucleon diameters. Two nuclear forces are involved, the strong and the weak interactions, differing in the magnitude of their force constants by a factor of about $10^{13}$. Furthermore, experiments with high-energy accelerators have revealed a disturbingly large complex of particles and excited particle states. New concepts and new conservation laws have had to be introduced to deal with these phenomena and their complicated relationships. Clearly, a more fundamental approach is required than the evidence of our senses or analogies based on the inverse-square forces.

The direction of this approach is toward an understanding of the most general basic symmetries in nature and the invariance principles which underlie the conservation laws we observe.

Each conservation law is a statement that some one physical quality or property is unchanged during all possible physical processes, such as in all interactions between particles, and is evidence of a more general invariance principle. An invariance principle is a statement that all laws of nature remain unchanged for some particular change of physical conditions, real or imaginary. Underlying each invariance principle is some basic symmetry of nature which determines the constraints which provide order to an otherwise chaotic world of particles. It is possible that the number of such symmetry principles is limited and that they are interrelated. When viewed from this aspect of the basic symmetries, nature may show a coordinated simplicity which is not visible in the great variety and complexity of conservation principles and physical laws which we observe.

## SYMMETRY OF SPACE

One of the most basic symmetry principles is that of the *homogeneity of space* and the associated *symmetry of time*. The symmetry of space includes both translational and rotational symmetry and applies to both stationary and moving systems. One consequence of the translational symmetry of space is the invariance of physical laws under translation from one location to another. An experiment to measure the mass of the electron should give the same result, whether performed in France or in California. This invariance of physical laws under translation implies the existence of certain conservation laws, specifically the conservation of energy and of momentum. The laws of motion also remain the same in a system moving at constant velocity, expressed by Newton's laws. For a system undergoing acceleration, the laws of motion are still valid when expressed in the appropriate formulations defined in the theory of general relativity.

The rotational symmetry of space determines the shapes or forms of allowed systems. The spherical symmetry of the gravitational field and of the coulomb field, which result in inverse-square laws for these forces, is a direct consequence of the rotational symmetry of space. The motions of the planets in our solar system and the shapes of their orbits were beautifully explained when Newton traced this symmetry to the spherically symmetric character of the gravitational force.

We observe many examples of space symmetry in nature, in crystals and in snow flakes; many living organisms, particularly microorganisms, exhibit perfect three-dimensional symmetry of form. The periodic table of the elements showed another type of symmetry even before its origin was understood. All these symmetries are now recognized as direct consequences of the isotropic character of the coulomb force between charged particles.

The mathematical representation of these symmetry laws takes on a symmetry of its own, with intrinsically simple and symmetrical formulations. The mathematical symmetry manifests itself in the coordinate-free form of the equations. Either all coordinate systems belonging to a certain class are physically equivalent, or the form of the equations is the same, for every one of the coordinate systems in the specified class. These invariance properties of the equations lead directly to the accepted conservation laws. For example, the invariant forms of the equations of motion lead to conservation of linear and angular momentum.

We are further guided in our search for symmetry by our growing understanding of and experience with the quantum mechanics. Quantum mechanics has introduced new basic principles and theoretical generalizations which have been extraordinarily successful in correlating and interpreting the phenomena of atomic physics. The quantization of energy in discrete energy levels, the existence of quantized momentum states, the wavelike property of material particles, and the uncertainty principle are aspects of a quantitative theory which explains and predicts atomic phenomena with high precision.

It summarizes in elegant mathematical language a great deal of our experimental evidence in the world of the very small. Quantum mechanics has also had major successes in correlating and interpreting the properties of nuclei, at energies millions of times greater than those of electrons in atomic states. These successes in prediction over such a wide field of phenomena and wide range of energy are fully supported by experimental confirmation and are evidence of the broad validity of the basic principles of quantum mechanics. They are also evidence for the rotational symmetry of space, which is the shape-giving property of nature.

At present, quantum mechanics is our best approximation to a theory of matter. However, it is by no means completely satisfactory. An impression is growing among theoretical scientists that some of the most basic concepts and premises must be changed in the sense that Einstein's theory of relativity changed the basic concepts of Newtonian mechanics. One of the weaknesses of quantum mechanics is that it does not and cannot predict the magnitude of basic constants such as the electron charge and electron mass from fundamental principles of the theory; these must be provided by experiment. Another weakness is in the philosophical interpretation of the limits to human knowledge associated with the uncertainty principle.

In quantum mechanics, energy is not an abstract or separable quality of matter but is closely associated with the shapes and the symmetries of atoms and nuclei. The states of lowest energy are those with the simplest of shapes and inherent spherical symmetry; they show up in the language of quantum mechanics as simple spherical harmonics; and they are demonstrations of the rotational symmetry of space operating through the spherical symmetry of the coulomb field. Higher-energy states in atoms or nuclei can have radial and axial components, but they also have the rotational symmetry of higher-order spherical harmonics. The law of conservation of angular momentum in atomic systems is a consequence of this symmetry of space.

## SYMMETRY OF TIME

The concept of time is closely associated with that of space. An event which occurs at a particular location in space and at a specific time can be considered to be a single point in "space-time." The "size" of this point in space-time is bounded by the uncertainty principle. In visualizing the interactions of particles we can think of paths through time as well as paths through space. The course of an interaction can be plotted on a graph of space versus time, with time as the ordinate. Particles entering or emerging from an interaction are represented by lines on the plot with slopes given by the velocities of the particles. A few space-time plots of typical particle processes are illustrated in Fig. 12.1. A particle at rest is a vertical line, with an arrow

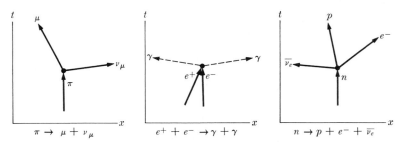

**Fig. 12.1** *Plots of particle interactions on space-time coordinates.*

pointing upward (positive) which represents time moving toward the point of the interaction. A particle moving with a velocity close to that of light, to the right in space, is shown by a nearly horizontal line with a small positive slope; another such particle moving to the left has a small negative slope. Entering particles are in the lower half of the plot with arrowheads pointing toward the point of interaction; product particles are in the upper half, pointing away from the interaction.

In discussing the world of the very small and very-high-energy particles, we must be prepared to consider the inner

structure of the event represented by the point in space-time.
We have indicated that this point has a "size" specified by the
uncertainty principle. If we expand this point on the space-
time plot we can insert lines or symbols representing our concept
of what actually happens in the course of the interaction. For
example, it is possible to conceive of the scattering of one electron
by another electron as involving the exchange of a photon. The
electromagnetic field theory does, in fact, include terms representing such a photon exchange.

A few such expanded-point processes are illustrated in
Fig. 12.2. Such a figure is called a *Feynman diagram*, in recog-

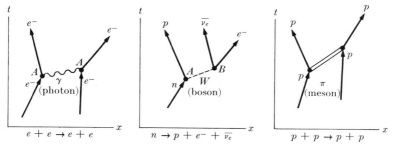

**Fig. 12.2** *Feynman diagrams showing possible coupling mechanisms
in interactions.*

nition of R. P. Feynman's early use of this technique to represent
pictorially the mathematical expressions in the field theory
which describe possible or alternate mechanisms of interaction.
The exploded view of an interaction in a Feynman diagram is
contained between two vertices which include between them the
"point" of the interaction in space-time. The dots labeled $A$
and $B$ on the diagrams in Fig. 12.2 are such vertices.

An additional feature added to the space-time diagram by
Feynman is the representation of antiparticles as lines with
their arrows reversed. The arrowhead is actually redundant,
since all particles move forward in time. Use of the reversed

arrowhead identifies the entering or emergent particle as being an antiparticle, while the location and slope of the line describe its role in the interaction. This symbolism is quite valid as a representation of the mathematics. According to field theory, the creation of a positron is equivalent to the annihilation of an electron. The mathematical description of a positron field propagating forward in time is the same as that of an electron field propagating backward in time. It is quite consistent, theoretically, to think of particles moving backward in time as well as forward.

The concept of particles moving backward in time has been quite useful in discussing the significance of the theoretical expressions used to describe particle interactions. It also provides a simple conceptual picture to "explain" the existence of antiparticles. In the theory of relativity there is nothing to prevent backward motion through time. The laws of physics are all framed in such a way that they are symmetrical in time and, in principle, a physical process can occur in the reversed direction as well as the forward direction in time. If antiparticles can be represented mathematically as particles moving backward in time, it makes some sense that they are so rare in our world in which time flows forward.

The evidence that time flows forward in our world comes only from our human faculties; we have a memory of time past, and our only experience is with time that flows forward. However, it is entirely consistent to conceive that time is symmetrical, for purposes of the theoretical study of particle interactions. Symmetry of time is an inherent property of our present theories, and the use of this feature of the theory has resulted in consistent descriptions of particle interactions and predictions which can be verified experimentally. There is no valid evidence (except our human senses) that time flows only one way. In the absence of such evidence the theorists in the particle physics field assume that there is a basic symmetry of time associated with the symmetry of space.

### SYMMETRY OF SPIN PERMUTATION

Quantum mechanics introduced another symmetry, that of the permutation or exchange of one particle with another in the electrons occupying energy states. The Pauli exclusion principle requires that a quantum state be antisymmetric with respect to such exchange. Two electrons can occupy a single state only if their intrinsic spins are opposed, but not if they are parallel. Since only two electrons can occupy the lowest state, others are forced into higher-energy states with different shapes. When combined with the properties coming from the spherical symmetry of the coulomb field, this *symmetry of permutation* leads to the known shell structure of atoms, the energy-level structure of the quantum states, and the grouping of energy levels into multiplets.

The symmetries of space and of permutation also apply to the shapes and structure of energy states in the nucleus, with the same consequences of shell structure and groupings of states into multiplets. Protons and neutrons are also fermions with spin $\frac{1}{2}$; the Pauli exclusion principle applies as for electrons. Only two protons with antisymmetric spins can occupy the lowest-energy state in a nucleus and others fall into higher states; the same is true for the first two neutrons. This group of four nucleons fills the lowest-energy level and forms a closed shell with spherically symmetric wave functions and shapes. The exceptional stability of the $He^4$ nucleus, which is observed as the $\alpha$ particle in radioactive decays, is conceived to be a direct consequence of these two basic symmetries. In heavier nuclei the additional nucleons enter higher-energy states with larger values of orbital angular momentum in which the basic spherical symmetry is still maintained; this leads to the observed shell structure of nuclei.

These symmetries of space and of permutation determine the general shapes of atomic and nuclear states and their groupings into energy levels. They do not, by themselves, determine the energies of these states or the magnitudes or extents of the wave functions. Magnitudes are determined by the strength and nature of the forces acting on the particles. In atomic systems this is the electromagnetic or coulomb force; the force constant comes from the experimentally observed forces between electric charges at rest and in motion. In nuclear physics the force is the strong nuclear force; the strength is determined by the observed nuclear properties such as the sizes and binding energies of nuclei.

The numerical magnitude of the force constant depends on the choice of units. In the cgs system of units the mechanical units of mass, length, and time are the fundamental quantities, and all other units (including charge) are expressed dimensionally in terms of these fundamental units. In the rationalized mks system of electromagnetic units, charge becomes a fourth fundamental quantity, and the proportionality constant in Coulomb's law is expressed in these four units. Experimental observations determine the magnitude of the force constant.

In atomic physics, observations of the magnitude of the energy changes and of the dynamics of interactions provide the evidence which determines the energy values of the atomic states. No theory has yet been able to predict these quantitative properties of atoms from the basic symmetries. They can be derived from the experimentally observed properties of the component particles such as their mass, spin, charge, and magnetic moments. The force constants for nuclear interactions also come from observations of the magnitudes of the interactions. The energies involved in nuclear processes are not calculable from any theory, from the intrinsic properties of the known particles, or from any of the consequences of the basic symmetries.

## SYMMETRY OF CHARGE PERMUTATION

Particle physics has added another symmetry of permutation, that of the charge states of particles involved in the strong

nuclear interactions, which is called *isotopic-spin symmetry.*
The evidence comes from the equivalence of nuclear forces between these particles, regardless of their charge. The first
example of this equivalence was in the experimental evidence
that the nuclear force between *p-p*, *p-n*, and *n-n* pairs is the same,
when corrected for the coulomb force due to the charge of the
proton.

This charge independence of nuclear forces indicates a basic
symmetry which leads to the existence of two charge states of
the nucleon. It is analogous to the spin-permutation symmetry
which allows two spin states of $\pm\frac{1}{2}$ for electrons in atomic states
or for protons and neutrons in nuclear states. This analogy
led to the name isotopic spin to describe the number of charge
states and to the parallelism in the use of mathematical symbols
and in theoretical calculations. The isotopic-spin symmetry principle describes an invariance with regard to rotation of a symbolic
vector representing charge, in a frame of reference (charge space)
which distinguishes the charge states. Since there are two
charge states for the nucleon, the vector can have two orientations, for positive and for zero charge.

With the discovery of the new unstable particles, isotopic
symmetry has brought into particle physics a multiplet structure
of charge states, similar to the multiplet energy levels which
spin-permutation symmetry brought into atomic and nuclear
physics. These multiplets contain particle states of different
charge which can be considered as substates of the same system.
The application of this new symmetry principle in particle
physics is even broader than its prototype in atomic and nuclear
physics. This complexity in the multiplicity of particle states
is discussed in Chap. 8, where it is shown to lead to states with
1, 2, 3, and 4 charge substates, distinguished by their isotopic-
spin quantum numbers. The unique feature of isotopic symmetry compared with the other symmetry principles described
above is that it applies only to the particles involved in strong
nuclear interactions.

## TCP INVARIANCE

In the search for a broader unity among the symmetries and invariance principles which apply to the particle world, theorists have proposed a more inclusive principle called *TCP invariance*. The letters stand for three hypothetical processes: T represents *time reversal*, the operation of reversing (mathematically) the direction of flow of time; C is *charge conjugation*, the technical term for interchanging particles and antiparticles in the theoretical expressions; P is *parity reversal* which involves space reversal or, loosely, taking the mirror image of the process. The TCP invariance theorem is essentially a conservation principle of a very broad type, which says that if these three mathematical operations are performed on the theoretical formulations of any physical process, the result is another physical process which is also allowed. The justification for the belief that this invariance theorem is valid goes far beyond the scope of this survey. However, it is involved in many of the most basic experiments on particles at the present time; in the reports of some recent experiments reference to the TCP symbolism has even appeared in the public press.

The breakdown of parity conservation in the weak interactions, discussed in Chap. 7, required a reevaluation of the TCP invariance principle. If parity is not conserved in an interaction, TCP invariance can hold only if another one of the operations is simultaneously not conserved. The theorist's answer is that the CP combination is still invariant and that charge conjugation must also be violated in weak interactions in which parity is not conserved. This requires that time reversal invariance be an absolute law. For the strong nuclear and electromagnetic interactions, C invariance and P invariance are still believed to be separately valid. But for the weak interactions only the combination CP invariance holds.

There is some experimental justification for this conclusion. For example, consider the decay of the $\pi^+$ pion

$$\pi^+ \rightarrow (\overline{\mu^+})_L + (\nu_\mu)_L \qquad (12.1)$$

where the subscripts $L$ indicate that both products are left-handed, as discussed in Chap. 7. If we perform the charge-conjugation operation C on this process, the effect is to change particles and antiparticles, which can be represented by

$$\overline{\pi^-} \xrightarrow{?} (\mu^-)_L + (\overline{\nu_\mu})_L \qquad (12.2)$$

This process is not possible, since the helicity is wrong for both products; so charge-conjugation invariance is violated. If we perform the parity operation P separately the effect is to reverse the spins or to convert $L$ to $R$ (right-handed) in Eq. (12.1). We get

$$\pi^+ \xrightarrow{?} (\overline{\mu^+})_R + (\nu_\mu)_R \qquad (12.3)$$

This process is also not possible, since helicity is again wrong for both products; parity conservation is violated. However, if we perform the C and P processes simultaneously, we have

$$\overline{\pi^-} \longrightarrow (\mu^-)_R + (\overline{\nu_\mu})_R \qquad (12.4)$$

This operation results in products with the correct helicities and is an allowed and observed process; so CP invariance is conserved.

Confidence in the validity of time-reversal invariance comes largely from the observed symmetries in the mathematical formulations of the general theory of particle interactions. If experimental observations were to demonstrate a violation of this principle, it would present a major challenge to some of the most fundamental aspects of modern theory. One experimental approach is to search for a possible asymmetry in the particle-antiparticle balance, which would be a violation of charge-conjugation invariance, in an interaction in which parity is conserved. This could be interpreted as meaning that time-reversal invariance is also being violated. One type of experiment is to search for asymmetry in the energies of the $\pi^+$ and $\pi^-$ pions emitted in the decay of the $\eta^0$ meson state

$$\eta^0 \longrightarrow \pi^+ + \overline{\pi^-} + \pi^0 \qquad (12.5)$$

If the average energies of the two charged pions are different, it would indicate an asymmetry in the particle-antiparticle balance. Experiments performed in different laboratories on this reaction have given contradictory results. At time of writing, there is still no solid evidence that T invariance is being violated.

### SU(3) AND SU(6) SYMMETRIES

In quantum mechanics the theory of groups plays a more important role than in classical theories because the states of a quantum-mechanical system form a linear manifold; that is, one can select a set of so-called basic states such that every other conceivable state of the system can be written as a linear combination of these basic states. This is not possible in classical theories. The states of a quantum-mechanical system are defined by the symmetries. For example, all the quantum numbers and quantum states of motion of an isolated system are determined by the group-theory representations of the symmetry of space-time. For interacting systems, the group representation provides a formulation useful in exploiting the symmetry properties of a basic principle which is too complicated to be susceptible to an exact solution.

We probably do not yet know all of the constituents and interactions of particle physics, but we do observe multiplets of particle states which apparently belong to symmetry groups. Group theory can be used to express the symmetry principle involved and may provide information on the missing members of a multiplet or on new systems of multiplets.

*Special unitary group theory* based on two fundamental states [known by the symbol SU(2)] leads to the prediction of a multiplet structure in the spectrum of substates. SU(2) theory for a system of two nucleons leads to the proton-neutron isotopic spin doublet ($I = \frac{1}{2}$) and also gives rise to singlets and triplets with $I = 0$ and $I = 1$. Group theory based on three nucleons

[SU(3)] gives rise to doublets ($I = \frac{1}{2}$) and quartets ($I = \frac{3}{2}$), etc.

A special application of SU(3) theory, which was developed by M. Gell-Mann and Y. Ne'eman, and which has had considerable success in recent years, is based on three fundamental states of the strongly interacting particles. These states cannot be identified with the known nucleons or other particles, but their properties are inferred from the observed number and characteristics of the known particle states. In the spectrum of baryons and baryon states known in 1964, there were isotopic-spin singlets, doublets, triplets, and quartets, which formed a pattern similar to that which would be expected from a trichotomy of three basic states. By working backward from this (incomplete) evidence, it was possible to infer the properties of the three states, which were given the name *quarks*. When the SU(3) expressions were "normalized" by using the properties of the known particle states and solved, they predicted another as yet unobserved singlet state with a mass higher than any of the existing states, a spin of $\frac{3}{2}$, and a negative charge. The $\Omega^-$ (as it was called) was searched for experimentally and promptly found with a mass essentially equal to the predicted mass.

This initial success of the SU(3) theory increased confidence that the correlations were meaningful. These correlations identified particles and particle states with the representations of components of the SU(3) theory, illustrated in Fig. 12.3. Here the basic *octet* of states is identified with the nucleon, the $\Sigma$-particle triplet, the $\Lambda^0$ particle, and the $\Xi$-particle doublet. The eight states form a symmetrical (and complete) pattern when plotted against the variables $I_3$ (isotopic spin) and $S$ (strangeness). These same eight states also form a pattern of ground states in the spectrum of baryon states given in Fig. 10.3 and are enclosed in a dotted oval to identify this octet of states associated in the SU(3) theory.

The SU(3) theory predicts the existence of another group of 10 excited states in the baryon spectrum (a decuplet), also illustrated in Fig. 12.3, using the variables $I_3$ and $S$. This

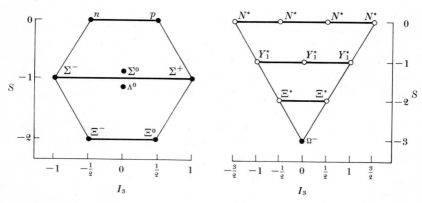

**Fig. 12.3**    *Group theory SU(3) representation of baryons and baryon resonances.*

decuplet predicted the existence of the Ω particle before it was discovered.   These 10 states are also enclosed by a dotted line in the spectrum of baryon states given in Fig. 10.3.

Another application of SU(3) symmetry is to the spectrum of meson states.   Here the theory predicts a basic octet of states and another octet of excited states, both of which are illustrated in Fig. 12.4, when plotted against the variables $I_3$ and $S$.   These

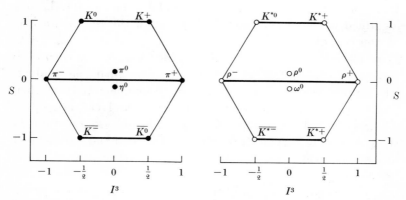

**Fig. 12.4**    *Group theory SU(3) representation of mesons and meson resonances.*

same groups are also enclosed in dotted ovals in Fig. 10.4, taken from Weisskopf's paper.

This success of the SU(3) theory in correlating the known particles and states is a strong indication that the symmetry of groups has some basic validity and significance. This system of symmetries is sometimes referred to as the "eightfold way" because it involves the operation of eight quantum numbers and results in groups of substates which are octets. The term eightfold way is a somewhat farfetched reference to an aphorism attributed to Buddha.

The significance of the three fundamental states called quarks which form the SU(3) group is by no means clear. Their properties are based on the properties of the particle states which they presumably form. Each baryon substate is conceived as a combination of three quarks, or parts of three quarks are needed to constitute a baryon. A quark-antiquark pair is needed to form a meson. The electric charge on the quark is either $\frac{1}{3}$ $q$ or $\frac{2}{3}$ $q$. Two of the quarks must have $I = \frac{1}{2}$ and $S = 0$ and the third $I = 0$ and $S = -1$. If quarks exist, they are more massive than baryons. When three quarks combine to form an observable baryon, excess energy must be released; yet there is no physical evidence of this energy. Whether quarks are real or virtual is unknown; whether their masses and lifetimes are within the range available for study with existing accelerator energies is also not known. Several laboratories have searched for quarks with no success. The term quark comes from an invented word in Joyce's "Finnegan's Wake."

The existence of two sets of particle states obeying the SU(3) symmetry in the baryon and in the meson spectra suggests that a wider symmetry might well be in effect. If instead of three basic states there are six, a broader symmetry principle based on SU(6) group theory might "explain" both spectra. This concept has been exploited with some initial success. The approach is to consider the quarks as having spin $\frac{1}{2}$ and to include a second set with spin $-\frac{1}{2}$. Quark-antiquark multiplets should exist with total spins 0 and 1, and the system of three quarks could have total spins of either $\frac{1}{2}$ or $\frac{3}{2}$. This later state predicts the tenfold group (decuplet) of resonances in the baryon spectrum. Another interesting result is the prediction of the magnetic moments of the substates; for the first time there is a theoretical basis for the ratio $\frac{3}{2}$ between the magnetic moments observed for the proton and the neutron.

The use of the symmetry of groups has been quite successful in correlating and ordering the great variety of particle states. The implication is that these many particle states represent a type of "fine structure" resulting from the interrelationships between entities of very much higher energy (and mass) than any with which we are so far familiar. The particle states we now observe with mass energies of the order of a few billion electron volts may be only the low-energy separations of substates of entities involving energies of 10 to 100 times greater. As Weisskopf remarks, "We saw a peak and thought it was the top of the mountain; when we climbed it we found ourselves facing the real top shrouded in dark clouds."

## TENTATIVE CONCLUSIONS

We can return to the question raised in the early chapters: What are the elementary particles? In one dictionary definition of the word *element* the first meaning is: "One of the simple substances or principles *formerly* believed to compose the physical universe." We italicize the significant word, since it is obvious that our concepts of what is elementary have undergone a continuous sequence of change. We no longer consider the 92 chemical elements as elementary but as well-defined assemblages of components which regenerate themselves under suitable conditions to the same basic shapes, based on the inherent symmetries of nature. Even the simplest of atoms are now considered to be composites of more fundamental particles.

Now scientists have raised the question in a deeper sense: What are the components of the elementary particles? They find growing evidence for a wide variety of forms in which energy can temporarily condense, which differ from each other in a systematic way depending on their individual quantum numbers, and which can be grouped into a limited number of families or types. The most significant result is that the similarities are more impressive than the differences between the individual particle states. The permanently stable particles (proton and electron) have only a minor form of uniqueness to distinguish them from the others; they can be considered the ground states of their particular families, but so can many others listed in the tabulation.

Let us approach the concept of "elementary" from the other side—by elimination. Some of the entities which we have listed as particles never appear as constituents of nuclei or other particles but are radiated or absorbed in transitions between states of different energy and with other different properties. The photon is the quantum of the electromagnetic field and never appears as a constituent of atoms or nuclei. Once radiated, the photon is presumably stable until it strikes another atom or nucleus in which its energy can be absorbed.

Neutrinos are also not constituents of matter, but are radiated (along with other leptons) in a variety of deexcitation transitions of nucleonic or particle states. In principle, the emission of a lepton pair including a neutrino is similar to the emission of a photon in that it carries away the surplus energy of an excited state as it transforms to a state of lower energy and in the process provides a mechanism for changing one or more of the quantum numbers. In this sense, neutrinos may not be elementary particles but rather radiations emitted to maintain conservation principles.

Mesons also fill the role of radiations in processes in which a state of higher energy transforms into one of lower energy with different quantum numbers. They fill this role in the strong nuclear interactions between the states in the baryon spectrum (Fig. 10.3) and in the meson spectrum (Fig. 10.4). One significant difference from photons is that mesons are known to occur in multiple-meson states such as the $\rho$, $\omega$, and $\eta$ resonances and are emitted as radiations in such multiple-meson states. Another obvious difference from photons or neutrinos is their finite and rather large rest mass. Nevertheless, the similarity between the deexcitation of atomic states by emission of photons and that of particle states by emission of mesons indicates some basic similarity in the two mechanisms. The meson must, in some fundamental way, be similar to the photon. The strongest evidence for this similarity is the fact that they are both bosons and obey the Bose-Einstein statistics.

At present, a promising theoretical approach is to conceive both the photon and the meson as quanta of fields. The photon which is the quantum of the electromagnetic field originates in the electric charge. It is believed that the active principle of the nuclear force is a mesonic field. Nuclear particles are conceived as continuously radiating and reabsorbing mesons so that at all times a meson field surrounds the particle. The extremely short range of the nuclear force is due to the large rest mass of the meson, which can be considered another aspect of the uncertainty principle of quantum mechanics.

Electromagnetic interactions can be expressed theoretically in terms representing the exchange of photons between electric charges and can be illustrated graphically by photon symbols between the vertices of a Feynman diagram. Strong nuclear interactions can be represented by the exchange of mesons between nuclear particles and illustrated by symbols representing an exchange of (virtual) mesons in a Feynman diagram. The concept of a field to represent an interaction has even been extended to the weak interaction in which the agency of this weak force is presumed to be a *vector boson* of unknown mass or other properties but which can be represented symbolically on a

Feynman diagram. The similarity of approach is due to these nuclear theories being based strongly on analogy with the electromagnetic field theory.

This survey is not the place to present the many alternative theoretical approaches to the problem of nuclear forces. These theoretical studies have developed in steps paralleling the growing evidence from experiments, but a general theory which includes the full complexity of particle states and their interactions has not yet been achieved. At present the approach is still phenomenological through experimental studies of the properties of particles and observations of their interactions. We are not working from a theory but to a theory. Recent theoretical advances, based on the generalizations possible from fundamental symmetry considerations, have had a measure of success. There is some hope that much of the evidence is now in hand and that the vague outlines of a general theory are appearing.

Returning to the question of elementary particles: Of the 100 or more particle states or radiations, the most significant aspect is the pattern of similarities they display, at least for the strongly interacting particles. Both baryons and mesons can be produced in several families of excited states, differing in their basic properties which are represented by the different quantum numbers. Each family has a lowest or ground state, but even these ground states are not permanently stable (with the exception of the nucleon doublet). Certainly the excited states or resonances are not elementary. The present analyses and tabulations suggest six baryon ground states and four meson ground states, with all but one in each category being charge multiplets. These are all essentially equivalent with the exception of the one permanently stable state, the proton. Without being too facetious we can paraphrase Orwell: "All particles are equally elementary, but the proton is more elementary than the others."

The pattern represented by the lepton states is not nearly so obvious. There is no theoretical understanding why muons exist; in all respects but their heavier mass they are similar to electrons. The significance of the pattern of four neutrinos with their different properties is also unknown. Possibly the concept mentioned above that leptons are primarily radiations emitted to maintain conservation principles may lead to a better understanding of leptons and their role in the weak nuclear force.

Particle physics is the study of these phenomena. The goal is a complete and basic theory of nuclear forces and particle interactions. A great deal is known about the facts and the experimental observations. The need for an inclusive theory is clear, and the time may be approaching when the basic principles of such a theory may be possible. However, some scientists feel that this theory may require a new fundamental structure of mathematics beyond any available at present, with an approach as radical and different as the step between classical physics and the quantum mechanics. Whether the human mind can conceive and formulate this new mathematics is a question for the future. Possibly some further major experimental discoveries are needed to point the way.

REFERENCES
FOR
FURTHER
READING

## Books presenting semipopular surveys in particle physics

ELEMENTARY PARTICLES, C. N. Yang (Princeton Univ. Press, Princeton, N.J., 1962).

THE WORLD OF ELEMENTARY PARTICLES, K. W. Ford (Blaisdell, 1963).

TRACKING DOWN PARTICLES, R. D. Hill (Benjamin, N.Y., 1963).

ELEMENTARY PARTICLES, A. M. Thorndike and D. H. Frisch (Van Nostrand, Princeton, N.J., 1963).

COSMIC RAYS, B. Rossi (McGraw-Hill, New York, 1964).

THE AMBIDEXTROUS UNIVERSE, M. Gardner (Basic Books, New York, 1964).

THE FUNDAMENTAL PARTICLES, C. E. Swartz (Addison-Wesley, Reading, Mass., 1965).

## Scientific American articles

| | |
|---|---|
| PIONS, R. Marshak | Jan., 1957 |
| THE OVERTHROW OF PARITY, P. Morrison | April, 1957 |
| ELEMENTARY PARTICLES, M. Gell-Mann and E. P. Rosenbaum | July, 1957 |
| THE PRINCIPLE OF UNCERTAINTY, G. Gamow | Jan., 1958 |
| ANTI-MATTER, G. Burbridge and F. Hoyle | April, 1958 |
| THE WEAK INTERACTIONS, S. B. Treiman | March, 1959 |
| HIGH ENERGY COSMIC RAYS, B. Rossi | Nov., 1959 |
| THE NUCLEAR FORCE, R. Marshak | March, 1960 |
| THE MUON, S. Penman | July, 1961 |
| THE SPARK CHAMBER, G. K. O'Neill | Aug., 1962 |
| NEUTRINO ASTRONOMY, P. Morrison | Aug., 1962 |
| THE NEUTRINO EXPERIMENT, L. Lederman | March, 1963 |
| CONSERVATION LAWS, G. Feinberg and M. Goldhaber | Oct., 1963 |

STRONGLY INTERACTING PARTICLES, G. Chew, M.
   Gell-Mann, and A. Rosenfeld                  Feb., 1964

THE OMEGA-MINUS EXPERIMENT, W. B. Fowler and
   N. P. Samios                                 Oct., 1964

VIOLATIONS OF SYMMETRY IN PHYSICS, E. Wigner    Dec., 1965

NEUTRINOS FROM THE ATMOSPHERE AND
   BEYOND, F. Reines and J. P. F. Sellschop          Feb., 1966

MUONIUM ATOMS, V. Hughes                  April, 1966

POLARIZED ACCELERATOR TARGETS, G. Shapiro      July, 1966

THE ORIGIN OF COSMIC RAYS, G. Burbridge        Aug., 1966

CAN TIME GO BACKWARD? M. Gardner           Jan., 1967

## *Physics Today articles*

| | | | |
|---|---|---|---|
| ON-LINE COMPUTER COUNTER AND DIGITALIZED SPARK CHAMBER, S. J. Lindenbaum | Vol. 18 | April, 1965 |
| THE STRUCTURE OF NUCLEONS, L. L. Foldy | 18 | Sept., 1965 |
| OF HIGHER SYMMETRIES, J. C. Polkinghorne | 18 | Oct., 1965 |
| PHOTOPRODUCTION OF MESONS AND HYPERONS, R. F. Bacher | 18 | Nov., 1965 |
| QUARKWAYS TO PARTICLE SYMMETRY, E. Wigner | 19 | Feb., 1966 |
| UNIFIED THEORIES OF ELEMENTARY PARTICLES, S. A. Bludman | 19 | Feb., 1966 |
| SPACE INVERSION, TIME REVERSAL, PARTICLE-ANTIPARTICLE CONJUGATION, T. D. Lee | 19 | March, 1966 |
| RELATIVISTIC QUANTUM FIELD THEORY, J. Schwinger | 19 | June, 1966 |
| HIGH ENERGY RESEARCH, G. W. Tautfest | 19 | July, 1966 |
| DEVELOPMENT OF THE SPACE-TIME VIEW OF QUANTUM ELECTRODYNAMICS, R. P. Feynman | 19 | Aug., 1966 |

*Special topics and surveys on a professional level*

TECHNIQUES OF HIGH ENERGY PHYSICS, D. Ritson (Interscience, New York, 1961).

PARTICLE ACCELERATORS, M. S. Livingston and J. P. Blewett (McGraw-Hill, New York, 1962).

QUANTUM THEORY & ELEMENTARY PARTICLES, V. Weisskopf (*Science*, **149**, Sept. 10, 1965).

ANNUAL REVIEWS OF NUCLEAR SCIENCE (Annual Reviews, Palo Alto, Calif.)

PROGRESS IN NUCLEAR PHYSICS (Pergamon Press, New York).

PROGRESS IN ELEMENTARY PARTICLE AND COSMIC RAY PHYSICS (Interscience, New York).

DATA ON PARTICLES AND RESONANT STATES, A. Rosenfeld et al. (*Reviews of Modern Physics*, **37**, 633, 1965).

# INDEX

Absorption lines, 36
Accelerators, multibillion-volt, 6, 79, 97
 particle, 4, 69, 70, 77
$\alpha$ particles, 15
Anderson, 63, 69
Ångstrom unit, 30
Angular distribution, 108
Angular momentum, 101
 in circular orbit, 33
 orbital, 104
Annihilation, 64, 83, 109, 189–191
Antiparticle, 63, 65, 83
 antikaon, 163
 antimuon, 72
 antineutrino, 66
 antineutron, 82
 antiproton, 82
 antiquark, 215
Associated production, 159
Aston, 20
Asymmetry, 58, 139
 (*See also* Parity)
Atomic mass unit (amu), 92, 118
Atomic radii, 34
Atomic spectra, 30–32
Atomic theory, 10
Average change, 166
Avogadro's number, 10

Balmer series, 30, 31
Baryon number, 85, 112
Baryon resonances, 179–180
Basic research, 2, 6, 7
Becker, 24
$\beta = v/c$, 92
Beta decay, 65–67, 197
$\beta$ particles, 15
$\beta$-ray transitions, 142, 143
Bevatron, 79
Bohr atom, 17, 30, 32

Bohr magneton, 105
Bohr postulates, 33, 54
Bohr quantization, 56
Born, 52
Bose-Einstein statistics, 42, 59, 218
Bosons, 59, 85
Bothe, 24
Brackett series, 31
Bubble chamber, 77, 98
 liquid hydrogen, 81, 158, 191
Butler, 80, 158

Canal rays, 18
Cathode rays, 11
Center of mass (CM), 43, 100
Chadwick, 24
Charge, electron, 14, 110
Charge conjugation, 210
Charge exchange process, 173
Charge independence, 149, 209
Charge-to-mass ratio, 12
 for ions, 20
Charge multiplets, 150, 209
Charge multiplicity, 178, 181
Cloud chamber, 98
CM (center of mass), 43, 100
Colliding beams, 98
Combination principle, 32
Combined state, 165
Compound states, 170
Conservation, of angular momentum, 100
 of charge, 110
 classical, 90, 114
 of energy, 90
 of isotopic spin, 152
 of linear momentum, 94
 of parity, 135
 of particle number, 112
 of strangeness, 160
 summary of, 185

Conservation laws, 90
Constraints, 148, 158
Cosmotron, 79, 158
Coulomb force, 26
Coupling constant, 26
  (*See also* Fine structure con-
    stant)
Cowan, 68
CP invariance, 210
Curie, 64

Dalton, 10
Davisson, 47
de Broglie, 47
de Broglie wavelength, 7, 52
Decuplet of states, 213
Democritus, 10
Dirac, 62
Disintegration of nuclei, 22
Doublet, 82
Doublet method, 22
Doublet states, 150
Doubly charged state, 151, 152
  (See also $N^*$ resonance)

Eightfold way, 215
Einstein, 5, 43, 46
Elastic scattering, 26, 171
Electromagnetic force, 4
Electromagnetic interactions, 192
Electron, 10
  charge of, 14, 110
Electron diffraction, 47
Electron family, 75, 113
  number, 114
Electron mass, 119
Electron neutrinos, 68
Electron-positron pairs, 111
Electron spin, 40, 59
Electron synchrotrons, 79
Electrostatic force, 26

Elementary particles, 10, 14, 84,
    216
  electron, 14
  neutrino, 67
  neutron, 25
  proton, 20
Elsasser, 47
$e/m$, 12, 20
Energy-level diagram, 36, 37
Energy states, allowed, 35
Energy width, 177
$\eta^0$ resonance, 179
Even parity, 134
  (*See also* Parity)
Excess mass, 5
Excitation function, 170
Excited states, 36, 170

Faraday, 10
Fermi, 66
Fermi-Dirac statistics, 58
Fermi transition, 142, 143
Fermions, 59, 85
Feynman, 205
Feynman diagram, 205, 218
Fine structure, 38
Fine structure constant, 26, 193
Fission, 5
Force constant, 208
Fresnel, 41
Fundamental particles, 62, 64
  (*See also* Elementary particles)
Fusion, 5

$\gamma$ rays, 15
  (*See also* Photon)
Gamow-Teller transition, 142, 143
Gardner, 70
Garwin, 140
Geiger, 17
Gell-Mann, 160, 165

Germer, 47
Goldstein, 18
Goudsmit, 40
Ground state, 36, 179
Group velocity, 49
Gyromagnetic ratio, 123

Hadrons, 88, 162
    quantum numbers for, 167
Heisenberg, 55, 149
Heisenberg uncertainty principle,
    55–58
Helicity, 131, 142
    left-handed, 139, 141, 144
    right-handed, 141, 144
He⁴ nucleus, 106, 207
Hertz, 11
Huygens, 41
Hydrogen spectrum, 31
Hypercharge, 166
Hyperons, 81, 112

Inelastic scattering, 172
Inertial mass, 46
    (*See also under* Mass)
Intrinsic spin, 24, 103
Invariance principle, 200
Ionization density, 99
Isotopes, 20
Isotopic spin, 149
    doublet, 149, 161
    nonconservation of, 154
    symmetry, 209
    third component of, 151
    triplet, 137, 161

Joliot, 64

Kaons, 81, 163
    decay of, 164–166
    doublet, 161

Kaons, mass, of charged, 126
    of neutral, 127
    (*See also under* Meson)
Kepler's laws, 102
Kinematic analysis, 174
Kinetic energy, 34, 92
    (*See also under* Energy)

$\Lambda^0$ particle, 80
    mass of, 127
Lattes, 69, 70
Laue patterns, 47
Lawrence, 64
Lederman, 140
Lee, 138
Left-handed helicity (*see* Helicity)
Length contraction, 45
Leptons, 74, 85
    number, 113
Lifetimes, 177, 179
    (*See also* Mean life)
Light, duality of nature of, 40, 57
    quanta, 41
    waves, 41
Lorentz, 11
Lorentz transformations, 43, 44
Lyman series, 31

McMillan, 77
Magnetic moment, electron, 106,
    122
    neutron, 106
    proton, 106
Magnetic quantum number, 39
    (*See also* Quantum number)
Marsden, 17
Mass, center of (CM), 43
    inertial, 46
    reduced, 35
    zero, 66
Mass difference, 121

Mass doublets, 22
Mass energy, 6
Mass spectrograph, 20
Mass spectroscope, 20
Mathematical symmetry, 202
Maxwell-Boltzmann statistics, 58
Maxwell theory, 41
Mean life, 178
Mendeleev, 10
Mendeleev periodic table, 16
Meson(s), 69, 85
    cloud of, 170
Meson field, 218
Meson resonance, 181
Millikan, 42
Millikan's oil drop experiment,
    13
Million electron volt (MeV), 4
    unit, 92, 118
Mirror image, 130
Mirror nuclei, 149
Missing mass, 93
Mole, 10, 92
Moment of inertia, 102
Momentum, 94
    (*See also* Angular momentum)
Multiple-meson states, 218
Multiplicity of states, 150
Muon, 69, 74
    range of, 74
Muon decay, 74
Muon family, 75, 113
    number, 114
Muon-mesic atom, 74
Muon neutrino, 68, 72, 75
Muonium atom, 75

Nagaoka, 14
Natural radioactivity, 15
Natural width, 178
Negative-energy continuum, 62,
    63

Neutral pion, 72
    mass of, 125
    (*See also under* Pion)
Neutrino, 67
    electron, 68
    muon, 68
    range of, 68
Neutrino mass, 124
Neutron, 23
Neutron mass, 121
Newton, 41
Nishijima, 160
$N^*$ resonance, 171, 173, 180
Nuclear emulsions, 73
Nuclear force, 4
Nuclear glue, 69
Nuclear magneton, 106
Nucleon, 27, 149
Nucleus, 17

Observable particles, 84
    number of, 88
Occhialini, 69
Octet of states, 213
Odd parity, 134
    (*See also under* Parity)
$\Omega-$particle, 82
    mass of, 128
$\omega^0$ resonance, 174, 190
Oppenheimer, 72
Orbital, angular momentum, 103,
    107
    quantum number, 38
    (*See also under* Bohr; *under*
        Quantum number)

Pais, 159, 165
Panofsky, 136
Parity, 133
    angular momentum term, 134
    conservation of, 136
        breakdown of, 138

Parity, intrinsic, 137
  reversal, 210
Particle physics, 3, 6
Paschen series, 31
Pauli, 65–66
Pauli exclusion principle, 40, 104,
  137, 187, 207
Pfund series, 31
Phase velocity, 49, 51
Photoelectric effect, 11
  quantum theory of, 41
Photon, 41, 85
  momentum, 96
Photoproduction, 193
Physical mass scale, 92
Pion, 69
Pion decay, 73, 194
Pion mass, charged, 124
  neutral, 125
Planck, 41
Planck constant, 41, 56
Positive ions, 18
Positive rays, 18
Positron, 63
Positron annihilation, 194
Positron mass, 119
Positronium atom, 109
Potential energy, 34
  (*See also under* Energy)
Powell, 69
Precession of spins, 140
Preferred spin orientation, 141
Principal quantum number, 33,
  36
  (*See also under* Bohr; *under*
    Quantum number)
Probability distribution, 55
  Born's concept of, 52
Proton, 18, 20
  radius of, 27
  stability of, 113
Proton mass, 120

Proton synchrotron, 79
Prout, 17, 18

*Q*-equation, 91
Quadruplet states, 150
  (*See also* Isotopic spin)
Quantum, 104
  of energy, 35
Quantum mechanics, 202
Quantum number, orbital, 38
  principal, 33, 36
  radial, 38
Quantum number strangeness,
  167
Quantum principle, 41
Quarks, 111, 213, 215

Radial quantum number, 38
  (*See also under* Quantum
    number)
Radiation pressure, 96
Radius of the proton, 27
Reines, 68
Relativistic kinematics, 100
Relativistic mechanics, 46
Resonance, 79, 170, 177
Rest mass, 45, 92, 118
  (*See also under* Mass)
Right-handed helicity (*see*
  Helicity)
Ritz' combination principle, 32
Rochester, G. D., 80, 158
Rotational symmetry, 201
Rutherford, 15, 17, 22, 23
Rydberg constant, 30–32
  for hydrogen, 36

Schrödinger wave equation, 51
  guiding wave described by, 53
Selection rule, 39
Shell structure, 106, 207
$\Sigma$ particle, 80, 127

Σ particle, mass of, 127
   triplet, 161
Signature, of decay processes, 175
   of a π⁻, 71
   of a π⁺, 75
Similarities, 217, 219
Singlet states, 82, 150
Soddy, 15, 16
Sommerfeld, 38
Space symmetry, 130
Space-time diagram, 205
Spark chamber, 76
Spatial wave function, 132
Special relativity, 43
Specific heat, 47
Spherical harmonics, 203
Spin, 24, 40
   correlations, 142, 145
   for Λ⁰, 146
   polarization, 144
Star, nuclear, 71
Stationary state, 33
Stevenson, 69
Storage rings, 97
Strange particles, 79, 158
Strangeness, 81, 161
   quantum number, 167
Street, 69
Strong interactions, 186
Strong nuclear force, 26
SU(3) theory, 212, 213
SU(6) theory, 212, 215
Symmetric wave function, 207
Symmetries, 59, 200
Symmetry, of spin permutation, 207
   of time, 204
Symmetry groups, 212
Synchrocyclotron, 79

TCP invariance, 210
"θ-τ puzzle," 138

Third component, 151
   (*See also* Isotopic spin)
Thompson, 11, 14, 18
Three-halves resonance, 154
Three-particle atom, 25
Threshold energy, 93, 97
Time, "dilated," 45, 72
Time reversal, 210
Time-reversal invariance, 211
Total angular momentum, 105, 106
Total energy, 34, 92
Translational symmetry, 201
Triplet states, 82, 100
Two-particle atom, 22

Uhlenbeck, 40
Uncertainty principle, 55–58, 204
Unitary group theory, 212

Valence electron, 40
Vector boson, 218
Veksler, 77
Velocity of light, 44
V tracks, 80, 98, 159

Wave function, 52, 133
Wave mechanics, 47, 57
Wave packet, 50, 53
Wave property of matter, 58
Weak interactions, 67, 138, 195
Weisskopf, 179, 215, 216
Wu, 138

Ξ particle, 128

Yang, 138
Y* resonance, 176
Yukawa, 69

Zeeman, 11
Zeeman effect, 40